# Gulf Oil Collectibles

Charles Whitworth

Schiffer Publishing Ltd
4880 Lower Valley Rd. Atglen, PA 19310 USA

# Dedication

This book is dedicated to my wife Hazel for allowing me to pursue my hobby of Gulf Oil Collectibles. I wish also to dedicate this book to the entire Gulf Oil family. To the service station attendants, the secretaries, management, the workers themselves in the oil fields, and to those who I may have left out unintentionally. If it wasn't for the fine family of Gulf Oil from 1901 to 1987, I would have no hobby. Many a person has given many years to Gulf Oil Corporation. I thank each and everyone of you. I would certainly be remiss if I didn't thank all of the many hundreds of individuals and dealers across the USA who have helped me to develop my collection.

The pictures in Gulf Oil Collectibles are from the author's private collection. The author always wants to hear from those who have worked for Gulf Oil Corporation or from someone who wishes to sell items relating to Gulf Oil. The author can be reached by writing to: Charles Whitworth P.O. Box 4073, Jeffersonville, Indiana, 47130.

When I really started collecting Gulf Oil, I had the help of Chris McKee and Wayne Henderson, two exceptionally knowledgeable historians on Gulf Oil. To these fellows and to the many others I have met, I thank you for the help you have given me. With this book it is hoped that you can enjoy the story in picture form of Gulf Oil Corporation. It is my hope to develop additional books on other items not covered in Gulf Oil Collectibles in the near future.

# Photography Credits

Roger Fisher, Photographer, Jeffersonville, IN 47130.


Library of Congress Catalog Card Number: 97-80817



*Designed by Bonnie M. Hensley*

ISBN: 0-7643-0505-0
Printed in China
1 2 3 4

Published by Schiffer Publishing Ltd.
4880 Lower Valley Road
Atglen, PA 19310
Phone: (610) 593-1777; Fax: (610) 593-2002
e-mail: schifferbk@aol.com Please write for a free catalog.
This book may be purchased from the publisher.
Please include $3.95 for shipping.

Please try your bookstore first. We are interested in hearing from authors with book ideas on related subjects.

# Contents

# Sign of the Orange Disc

## by Wayne Henderson

A recreation of Houston's famed Astrodome, in miniature. A lighthouse in Miami. A spectacularly flowing scalloped roof station at Atlanta's Hartsfield Airport. Elaborate structures at the end of busy viaducts in Pittsburgh and in dignified residential neighborhoods in Louisville, Richmond, Charlotte, Jacksonville, and elsewhere. A cute little four level "cottage" in a Virginia peanut town. A single orange pump in front of a country store in the Smoky Mountains. And, of course, a small, irregularly shaped brick building at Baum Boulevard and St. Claire Ave in Pittsburgh, where it all began.

Such are the images of Gulf. Almost 100 years ago, in 1901, fate was dealing a series of interesting hands to a group of pioneering oil men that were busy poking holes in East Texas. From this effort, random and haphazard, at a place called Spindletop, Gulf was born. Mellon money, from Pittsburgh's famed banking family, funded explorers James Guffey, Anthony Lucas, and John Galey. From their efforts, in May of that year, the J. M. Guffey Petroleum Company was created. The success of the early exploration led to construction of a Gulf Coast refinery at Port Arthur, Texas, and from the location, the name Gulf Refining Company was chosen in November of 1901.

The early years saw repeated successes, and an occasional failure, in the oil exploration game. Refining and marketing, however, grew at a slow but comfortable pace. Kerosene was the primary product, and Gulf Refining marketed theirs from tank wagons painted a distinctive orange. Other products and other markets were being considered when the two existing companies, Guffey Petroleum and Gulf Refining, were merged to form Gulf Oil Corporation in 1907.

The next several years saw a rapid expansion, as Gulf products were now marketed from Maine to New Mexico in an arc that included all or part of 29 states. The crowning achievement from such early success at Gulf was the construction of the world's first "built for that purpose, off-street gasoline filling station" opened December 1, 1913, at Baum Boulevard and St. Claire Ave in Pittsburgh, dispensing what was known as "That Good Gulf Gasoline." It would be the first of many, and by now control of Gulf was maintained with the other Mellon interests in Pittsburgh, so many of the earliest stations were constructed in and around the city. During the following year, as these additional outlets were opened, Gulf pioneered another gasoline marketing concept...free, branded road maps.

This effort, the opening of a chain of "filling stations," was definitely the wave of the future, and shortly thereafter many other refiners copied the Gulf concept. Each was determined to establish an identity uniquely their own. As Gulf expanded from the industrial base, in which its products were already known, into the retail market, the marketing image they selected was so successful that it continues, in modified form, even today. The image is that of the orange disc. Originally registered as a trademark in 1920, the logo has gone through a series of evolutionary changes, from border and lettering styles in the 1920s, to standardization in 1936, to other modifications in 1954 and 1960, and to the version still seen today that was created in 1963. Many of the items in this book will show the many ways that the orange disc with the blue block letters has always meant Gulf.

From the pioneer days, Gulf settled into successful steady operations, with Gulf facilities found in every town in their 29 state marketing area. In 1926 Gulf introduced an ethylized, higher-octane companion to "Good Gulf," known as Gulf "No Nox." These gasoline trademarks would continue in use for most of the next sixty years. Lubricants marketing became a focus as well, and in 1928 Gulf introduced Gulfpride, one of the most famous motor oil trademarks ever used by the gasoline marketing segment of the industry and a brand that is still available today. The thirties saw Gulf with more refining capacity, a slightly enlarged territory, and larger, better-appointed gas stations. Most Gulf stations were leased to independent dealers, given them a certain pride of local control that other gasoline marketers would imitate time and time again. Station design evolved, from the "sandbrick" or "tapestry" stations of the 1910s and 1920s, through modern brick outlets of the 1930s, into the "icebox" era beginning about 1940. Many of the older stations saw their elaborate brickwork covered in white porcelain with blue accents, an image forever associated with Gulf. Even today, one can still find an "icebox" Gulf station beckoning passing motorists with nostalgically gleaming white and blue porcelain.

Gulf operations survived the war and contributed to the effort, and in the postwar boom focused more and more on the retail marketplace. A complete line of automotive chemicals and accessories, as well as numerous household products, were introduced. For a short time Gulf even marketed major appliances under their own trademarks. Tires and batteries were big items as well, and dealers were encouraged to sell only the house brand. From this effort, from 1946 until the first gas shortage of the 1970s, the Gulf trademark would appear on a wider variety of products than those of any other gasoline marketing competitor. Other marketers such as Texaco, Shell, and Phillips, would imitate the effort, but no one gasoline marketer ever had marketplace acceptance to match Gulf. Even today, Gulflite Charcoal Lighter Fluid and Gulfwax are on the shelves in our local supermarket, although now under different ownership.

The 1960s and the price wars, often caused by Gulf's sub-regular grade "Gulftane," would bring an uneven financial picture for Gulf. Reaching out to new markets to help stabilize cash flow in this uncertain era, Gulf purchased marketing in various areas. First came Wilshire, purchased in 1960 and converted to Gulf in 1965. Discount operations Supreme 400/Coryell 70 and Bulko helped solidify the market in the urban areas of the upper Midwest. A purchase of hundreds of stations and jobber contracts from Cities Service in the mid-1960s brought the Gulf brand into areas that it had never before appeared. By 1970, the Gulf logo was to be found in all 48 continental states. With the 1970 purchase of Canada's British American Oil Company, Gulf signs replaced the BA and Royalite brands all across Canada. The occasional Gulf lollipop sign from the 1920s, found at a country store here in Western North Carolina, could be contrasted with Gulf signs now seen at remote trading posts along the Alcan Highway and in the Yukon.

The 1970s, with the gas shortages, were hard on many gasoline marketers, and Gulf perhaps suffered more than most. With their resources concentrated in only a few areas of exploration, Gulf had been secure in this concept until the nation of Kuwait nationalized oil exploration holdings in 1975, in which Gulf formerly had controlling interest. The loss is one from which Gulf would never recover. Forced to buy crude oil on the open markets to feed its refineries, Gulf closed facilities and abandoned entire portions of their marketing area, states where they had never been particularly profitable. In spite of the drastic cutbacks, Gulf, as a corporate entity, was doomed. In a spectacular stock-trading battle involving corporate raider T. Boone Pickens, Gulf disintegrated in 1984, with the majority of the company being purchased outright by Standard Oil Company of California–Chevron. We say disintegrated, as Chevron was forced to sell off certain marketing assets to avoid anti-trust action. In the southeast, where Chevron already had a foothold from their 1961 purchase of Standard Oil of Kentucky, the entire Gulf marketing network; terminals, bulk plants, and stations, jobber and dealer contracts, were sold to BP. BP had entered the US market in 1969 with the merger with Standard Oil of Ohio, and BP branded stations were found along the eastern seaboard, where BP had purchased many of the former Sinclair outlets. With a concentrated market only in Ohio, where the Sohio brand reigned supreme, BP was free to purchase the brand. In the mid-Atlantic region, and in Texas, many of the Gulf properties were converted to Chevron. In the northeast, where Chevron had continued from their Calso marketing established in the 1940s, the Gulf facilities were sold to a convenience store marketer known as Cumberland Farms. By 1990, the southern based BP controlled market was being converted to the BP brand, and today the Gulf brand survives only in the continuation secured in the Cumberland Farms effort, now known as Gulf Oil Limited Partnership. Gulf branded stations can still be found from the northern tip of Maine to points as far south as Delaware and along the Ohio River in Ohio. Gulfpride Oils are still available, and after almost 100 years of petroleum products represented by the color orange, the orange discs with the blue letters still proclaim to all the brandname Gulf.

Many of you know that I have collected petroleum memorabilia for most of my life. In the summer of 1963, when I was about a year and a half old, Dad took a block of wood left over from the construction of a picket fence and painted a little Gulf sign on it for me. I had wanted a little Gulf sign since the station in front of our mobile home fascinated me, even at that early age. Without the attraction of the Gulf logo, perhaps I never would have noticed. I owe my profession and my life's work, all the books, *Petroleum Collectibles Monthly*, all the effort, to a toddler's interest in an orange disc.

# Gulf Oil Collectibles

## Adhesives

1979 paper label quart, value $20 each.

1979 paper label quart, value $20 each.

1979 paper label gallon, value $25.

1978 cartridge, 30 oz., value $15.

Cartridge, 30 oz., 1978, value $12.

Cartridges (left to right) 1976, 1980, 1979, 1967, 1967, 11 oz., value $12 each.

All 1975 cartridges, 11 oz., value $12 each.

## Aircraft Engine Oil

Quart, metal, 1959, value $50.

Quart, 1962, value $40. Gallon, 1963, value $70.

Air filters, 1968, value $10 each.

## Antifreeze

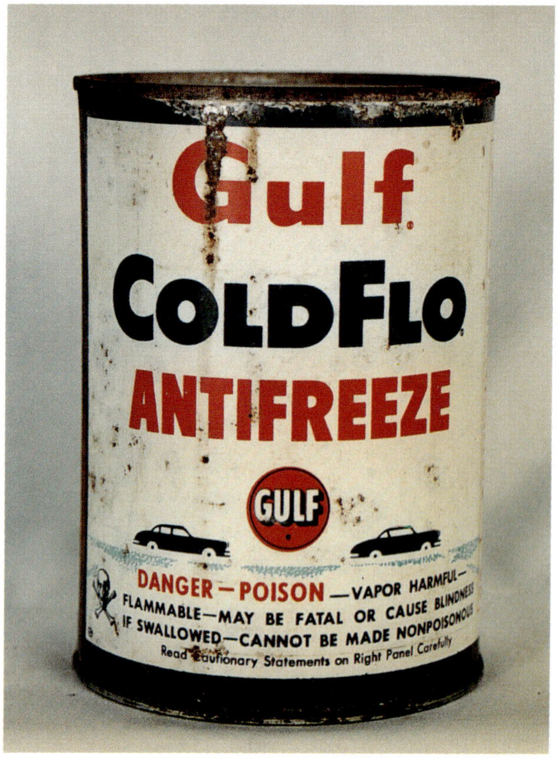


Metal quart, 1962, value $70.

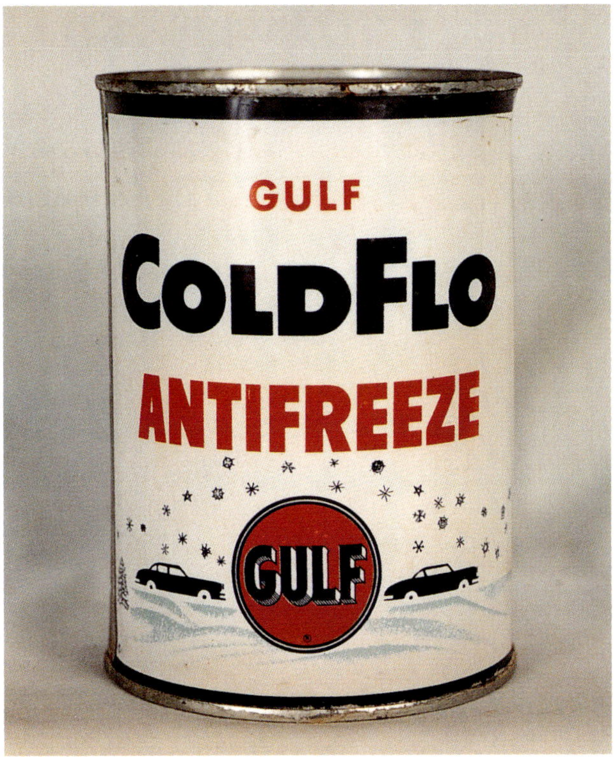


Metal quart, 1961, value $70.

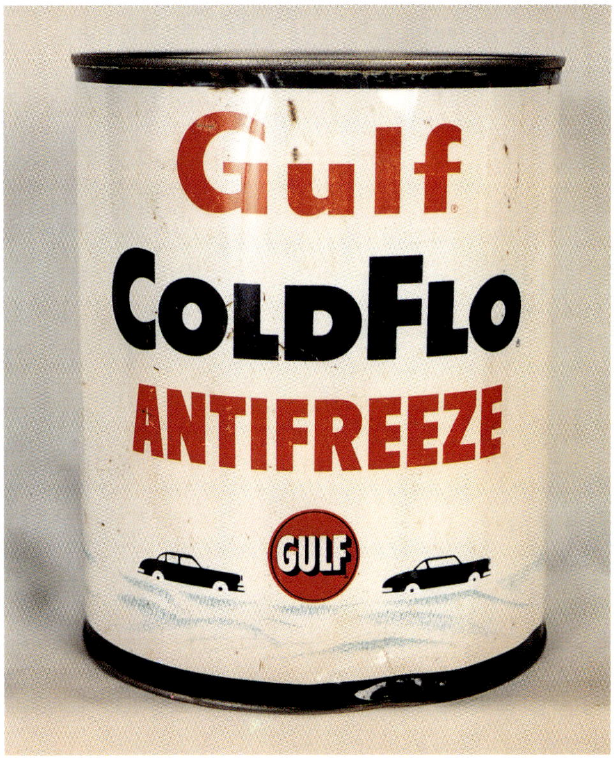


Gallon, 1960, metal, value $90.

Quart, 1962, value $70.

Gallon, 1961, value $90.

1956 gallon, value $80.

Gallon, 1962, value $80.

Antifreeze wire tag, 1958, value $8.

1964 metal gallon, value $65.

Quart, 1969, metal, value $50. Gallon, metal, value $80.

Quart, 1969, metal, value $50. Gallon, metal, value $80. (Other side of top photo.)

1948 round metal gallon, value $80.

1950 round metal gallon, value $85.

Quart, metal, 1959, value $70. Gallon, round metal, value $90.

Plastic gallon, 1974, value $15.

## Ant & Roach Killers

1961 display and 16 oz. metal spray bomb, value $15 and $25.

16 oz., 1959, value $30.

15 1/2 oz., 1970, value $12.

15 1/2 oz., 1974, value $12.

14 oz., 1965, value $20.

## Auto Filters

1968 fuel and oil filters, value $10 each.

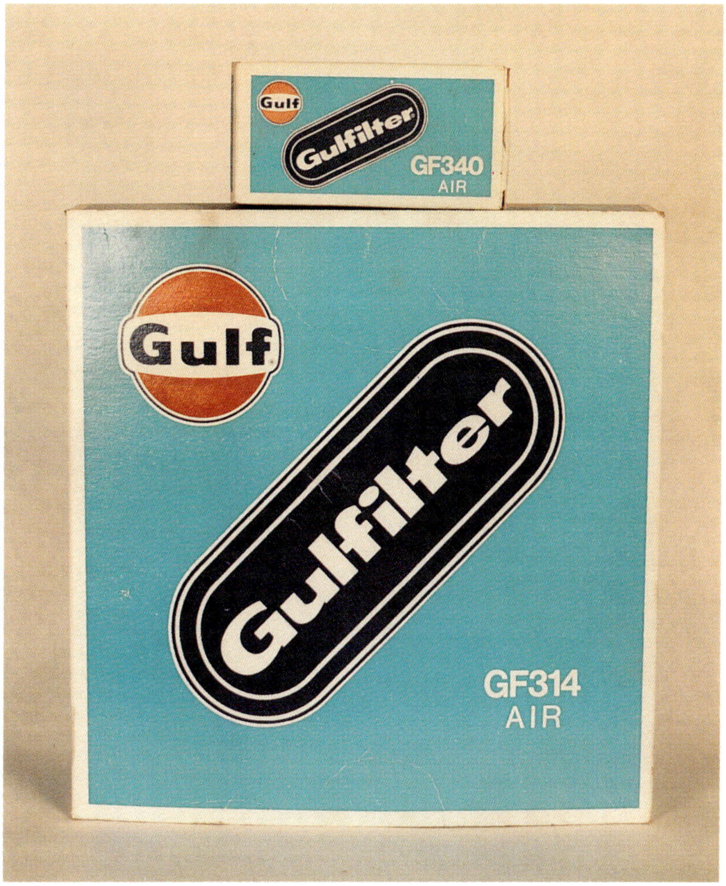

# Automatic Transmission Fluid

Paper quart, 1982, value $18. Plastic quart, 1982, value $20.

Paper quart, 1968, value $12.

Paper 1964 type-A quart, value $12.

Paper 1969 Dexron quart, value $12.

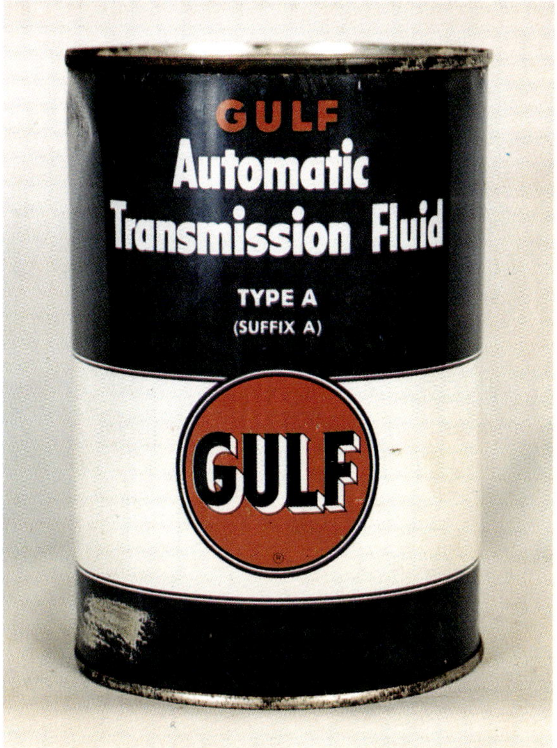


Metal quart, 1958, value $25.

1990s Plastic quart, value $5 each.

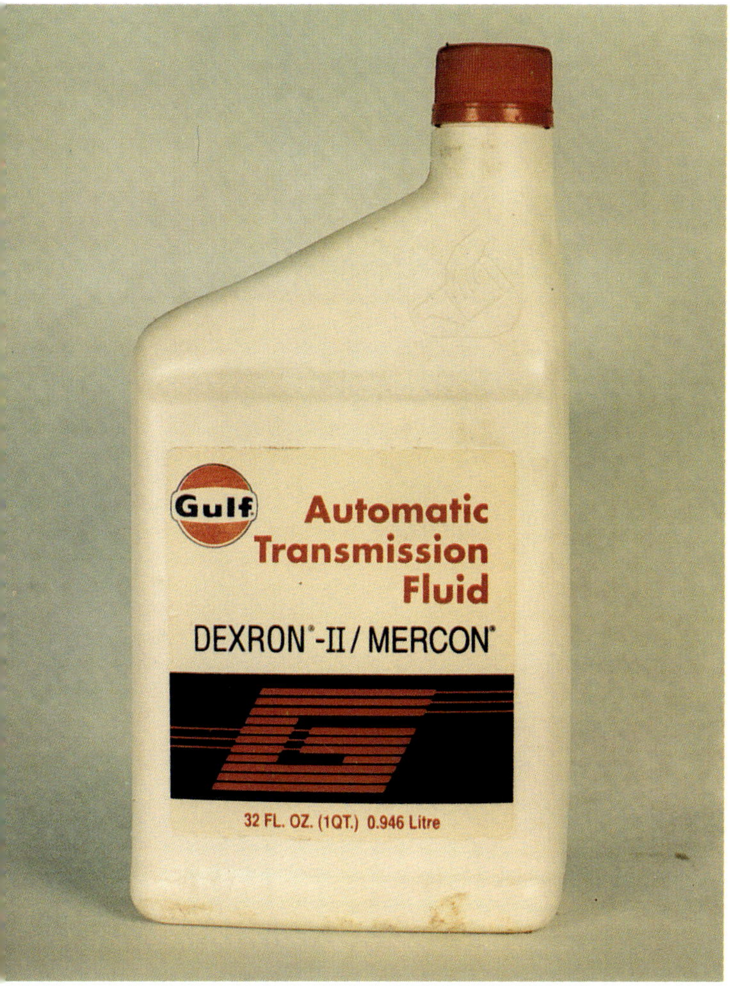


Plastic quart, 1990s, value $5.

Plastic Cumberland Farms BP, quart, 1996, value $5.

# Aviation Oil

Metal quart, 1951, value $55.

Metal quart, 1959, value $55.

Paper quart, 1983, value $20. Plastic quart, 1983, value $25.

Paper quart, 1969, value $70.

1961 Metal quart, value $65.

1949 Metal gallon, value $105.

Metal quart, 1950s, value $80.

# Banks

Paper coin banks, value $105.

Paper coin banks, value $120.

Plastic coin banks, value $25 each.

Plastic 6" tall coin bank, value $80.

Collector Series #2 Airplane Bank, value $85.

Collector Series #1 Airplane Bank, value $100.

## Battery Cables & Accessories

12-volt Battery cable, 1950s, value $22.

6-volt battery cable, value $25.

Nekrode Battery Cable, 1940s, value $20.

Battery cable, 1964, value $8.

Booklet Power Crest Batteries, value $15.

Battery service carryall, value $80.

# Brake Fluid

12 oz., 1951, cone top, value $30.

Gallon, metal, 1962, value $60.

12 oz., 1972, cone top, metal, value $30.

1968 one gallon, metal, value $50.

16 oz. metal, 1953, value $35.

One gallon, 1948, value $80.

Pint, early '40s, metal, value $70.

## Bug Killers

Pint, 1969, metal, value $20. Quart, 1969, metal, value $32.

Outdoor fogger, 16 1/2 oz., value $12.

Pint metal can, value $18.

# Buttons & Credit Cards

Various buttons, value range $12 to $20.

Various credit cards, value range $18 to $35.

# Car Care Products

One pound size, 1958, value $40.

One pound size, 1966, value $40.

One pound size, 1953, value $40.

Pint, value $15.

Pint metal can, value $20.

Glass bottle, 1940s, pint, Gulf Refining Co. embossed in glass, value not established.

One pound size, 1948, value $40.

Treated polishing cloth in metal container, value $45.

7.5 oz. glass container, 1945, value $40.

8.0 oz. metal can, 1949, value $40.

Pint, 1951, paper label, value $40.

One pound metal can, value $30.

One pound metal can, 1949, value $45.

Pint metal can, 1952, value $12.

Pint metal can, 1949, value $20.

Cleaner for tar removal, 1965, value $20.

# Charcoal Starters

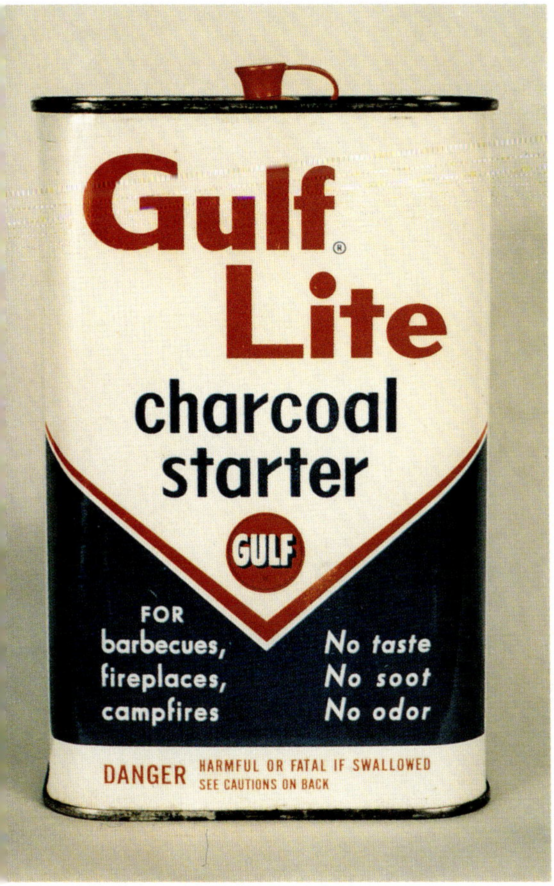


Pint metal can, 1961, value $25.

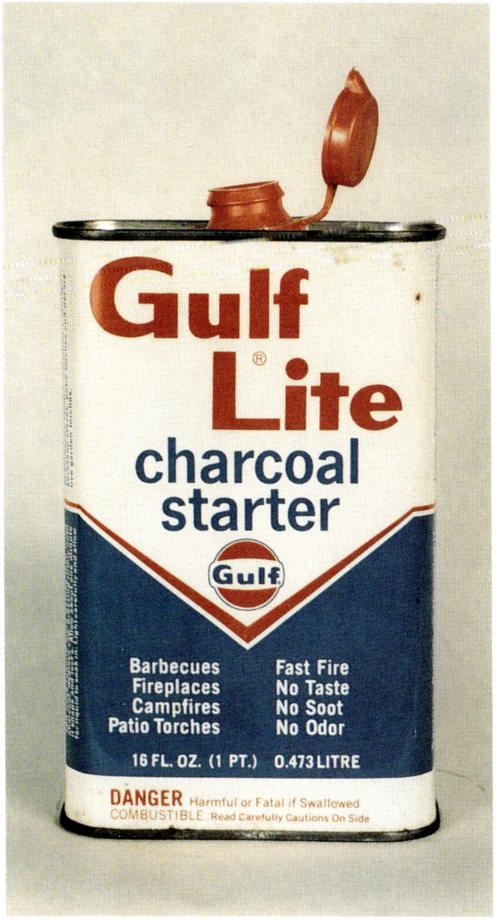


Pint metal can, 1980, value $10.

Plastic package, 1982, value not established.

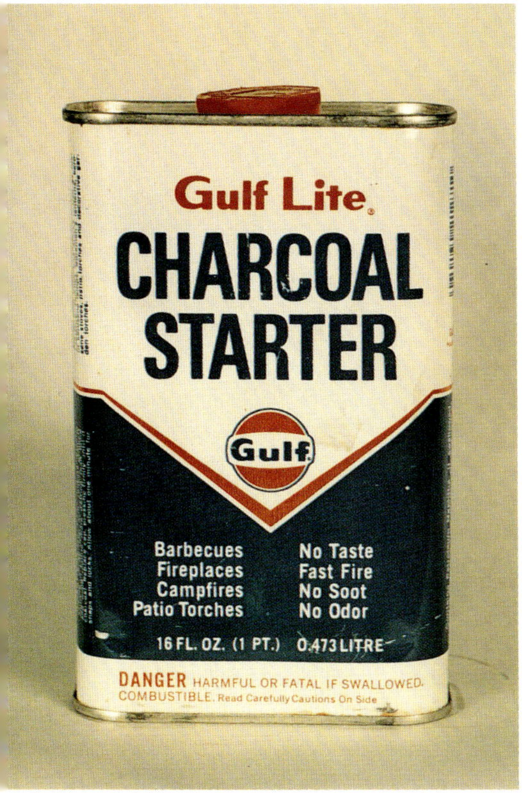


Quart metal can, 1975, value $12.

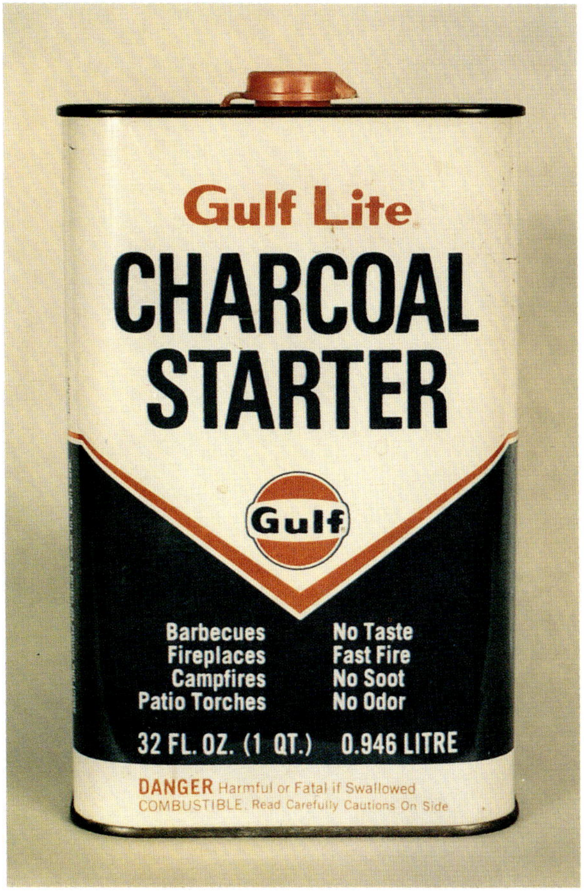


Quart metal can, 1971, value $10.

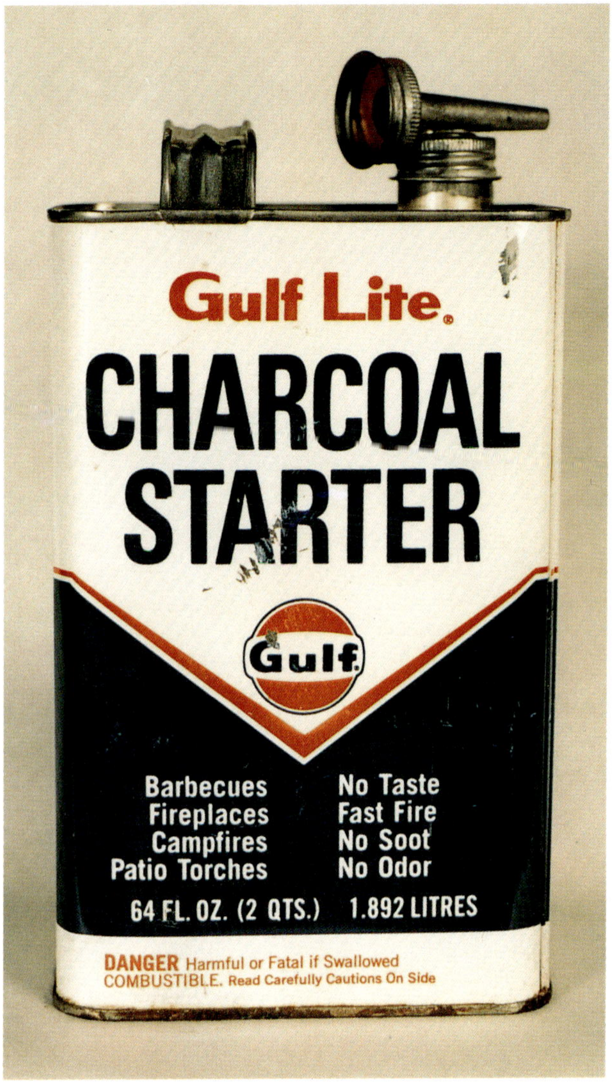


64.0 oz. metal can, 1971, value $20.

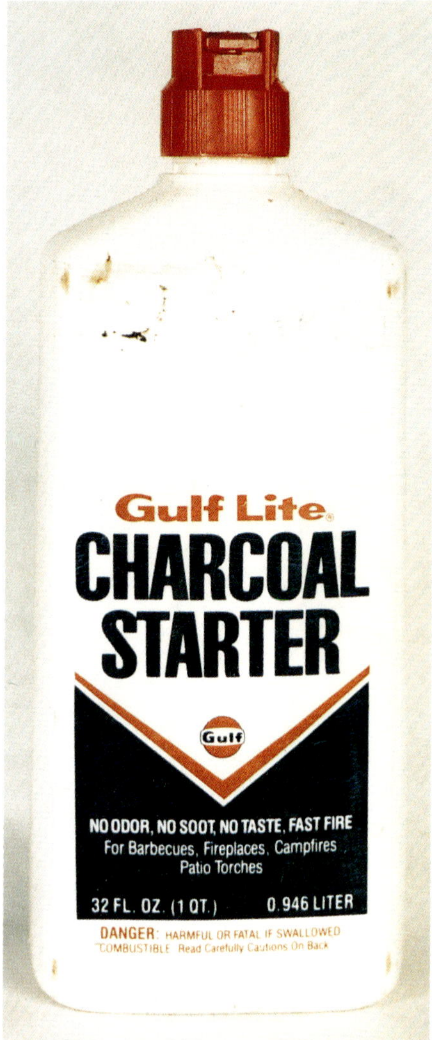


Quart, plastic, 1980, value $15.

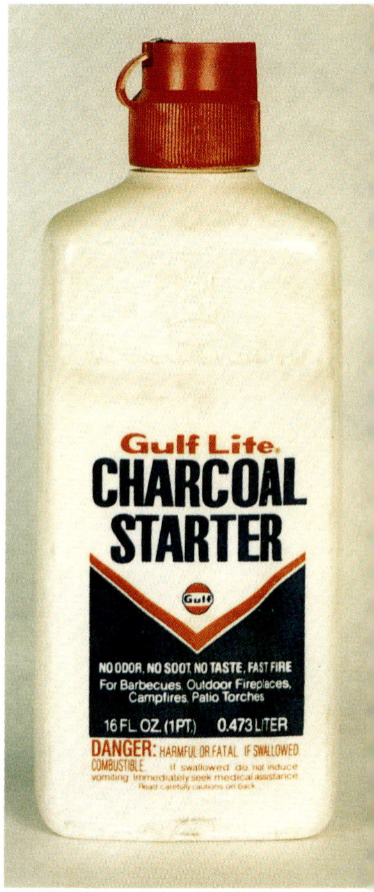


Pint, plastic, 1981, value $15.

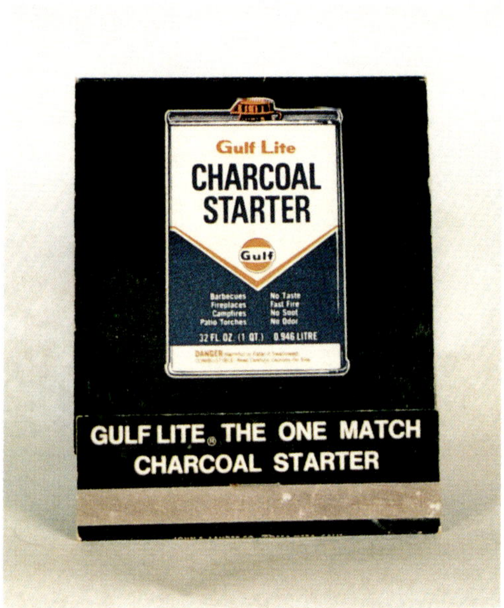


Match book cover with matches, value not established.

Match book cover with matches exposed, value not established.

## Clocks & Watches

Alarm clock, value $100.

Service station dealer clock, value $175.

## Clothes

Station attendant hat, value $100.

Station attendant grease hats, value $25.

Station attendant wearing hat, shirt, and blue pin-striped pants, complete outfit $300.

Baseball hat, value $8. Jacket $20.

Baseball hat, $8. Shirt, short sleeve, 1978, $15.

Baseball hat, value $8. Station attendant jacket, $20.

Dress shirt, value $20, hat $8. Hand-held sign saying Free Gifts on one side and Gulf on other side, $45.

Service attendant orange pin-striped pants, $200.

Gulf Kerolite jacket and toboggan modeled by photographer Roger Fisher, value not established.

Short-sleeve shirt, value $18. Hat, value $8.

Service attendant jumpsuit, value $90. Baseball hat $8.

Service station attendant white shirt, hat, and striped pants, value $200.

# Cups/Glasses/Dishes/Mugs/Silverware

Various glasses and cups, value $10 to $25.

Variety of three different glasses as promotional giveaways in 1987, value $3 each.

Various cups, value $3 to $10.

Tall drinking glasses showing the 5 different scenes to make a set, value $3 each.

Paper drinking cups used in cup dispenser in Gulf stations, value $3 each.

Gulf pewter mug, 1981, shown front and back, value not established.

Samples of silverware and dishes with Gulf emblem, prices vary.

## Door Ease

Door Ease display box used in Gulf Stations, value $20.

Metal tube, 1951, value $15.

Metal tube, 1969, value $15.

# Electric Motor Oil

Glass 4 oz. bottles, values $25 each.

Half pint, 1949, metal, value $20.

Metal, 4 oz., 1953, value $15.

Metal, 2 oz., value $55.

Half pint, metal, 1945, value $30.

One gallon, 1949, value $45.

## Farm Grease

Metal, 1957, value $25.

Metal, 5 pounds, 1960, value $25.

**Metal,** 5 pounds, 1963, value $25.

## First Aid Kits

Plastic, 1983, kit, value $40.

Metal, 1953, kit, value $45.

Metal, 1975, kit, value $45.

## Five Gallon Containers

1930s wooden crate to protect five gallon tin cans, value $45.

Wooden crate to protect five gallon tin cans, value $80.

Five gallon tin, value $45.

Oil to polish horse hooves, value $45.

1983, metal, value $25.

1953, metal, value $40.

1960, metal, value $45.

1954, metal, value $35.

Metal, 1920s, tin, 5 gallon, value $55.

# Flying Insect Sprays

12 oz., two versions of 1972 spray aerosol cans, value $12 each.

12 oz., two versions of 1968 spray aerosol cans, value $12 each.

Left, 1969 version, value $12. Right 1962 version, value $20.

Left, 1968 version, value $14. Right 1975 version, value $12.

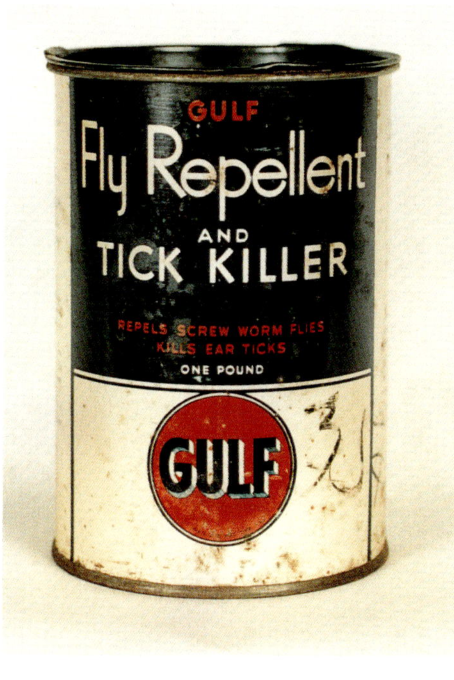


Metal, one pound, 1940, value $40.

Paper, one pound, 1946, value $50.

# Foreign Oil

Saudi Arabia metal quart, value not established.

Dubai metal quart, value not established.

Plastic litre, Chile, value not established.

Kuwait metal quart, value not established.

Korean metal quart, value not established.

Canadian 4 oz. handy oiler, value $40.

Canadian paper quart, 1983, value not established.

Canadian paper quart, 1983, value not established.

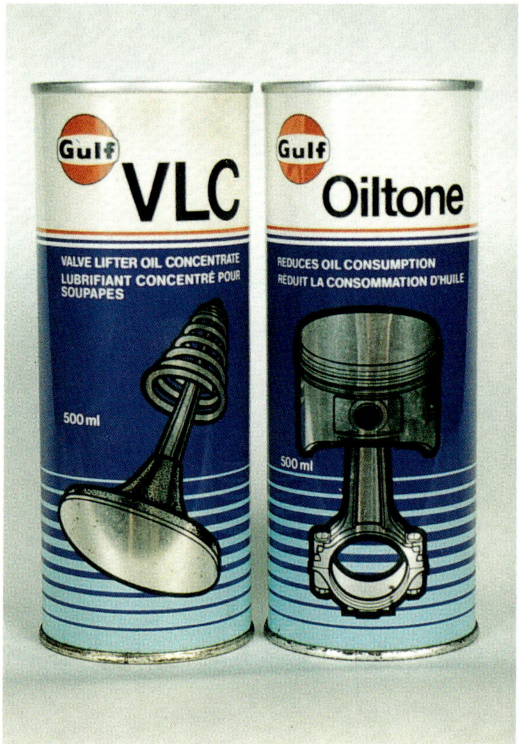


Canadian, 1983, value not established.

Canadian, 1983, value not established.

Canadian Imperial quart, value not established.

## Friction Tape

Display box, 1953, value $70.

Friction tape, 1953, value $15.

# Furniture Polish & Repair

Glass bottle, 1938, value $75. Metal, 1935, pint, value $90. Quart, value $100.

1938 Gulf Gleam, 8 oz., value $75.

4 oz. wood filler, value $30.

Glass bottles, 8 oz., 1950s, value $40 each.

# Gas Cans, Spark Plugs, Gas Caps, Oil Breathers

One-gallon gas can for Model T running boards, value not established, front view.

Rear view of one-gallon gas can for Model T running boards.

1972 oil breather vent cap, value not established.

1972 radiator safety pressure cap, value $75.

1972 gas cap, value $50.

1972 spark plug and box, value not established.

# Giveaways & Promotional Advertising Items

1980s golf balls, set of three in box, value $45.

Yo-yo, 1958, value not established.

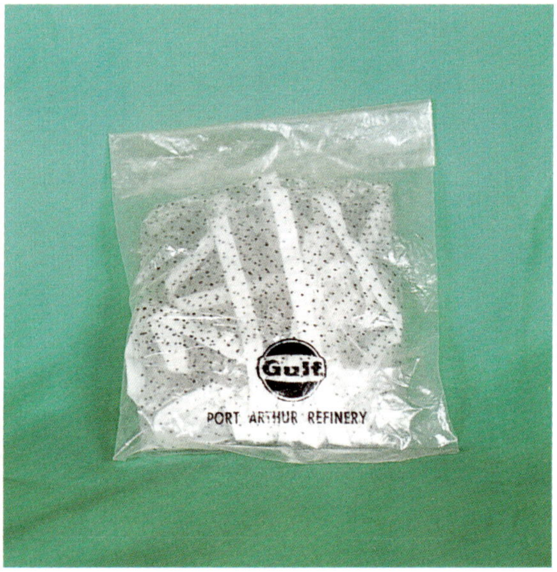


Woman's rain bonnet, value $7.

Golf towel, shoe horn, ball markers, and tees as a set, value $45.

Nolan Ryans commemorative baseball for most strikeouts, value $20.

1983 promotional kit with comb, hair tonic, facial tissue, sunburn cream, value $65.

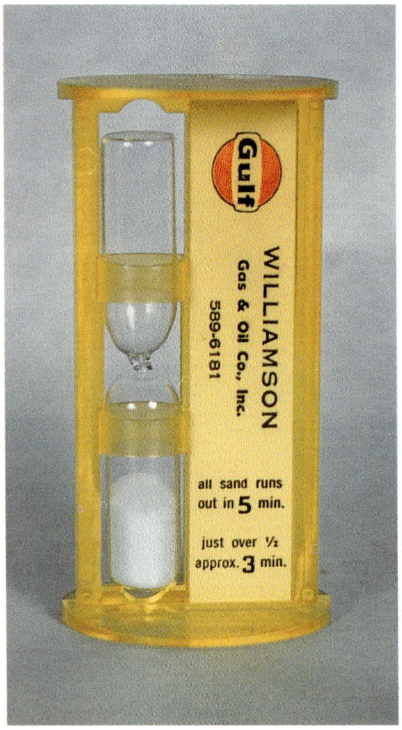


Egg timer, value $10.

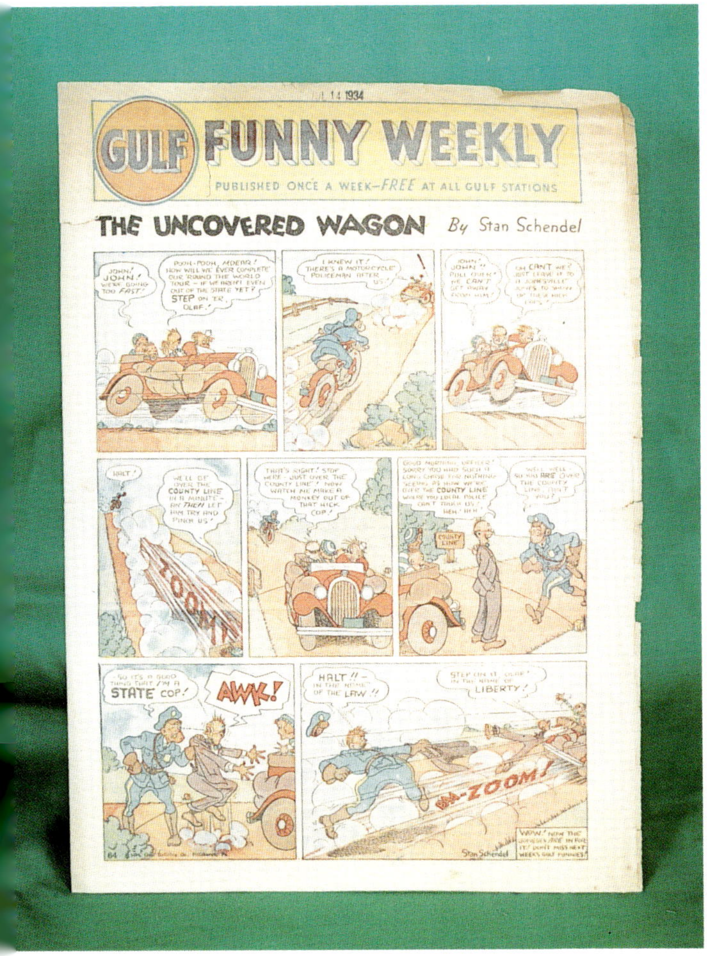


1934 issue of Gulf Funny Weekly, value $35.

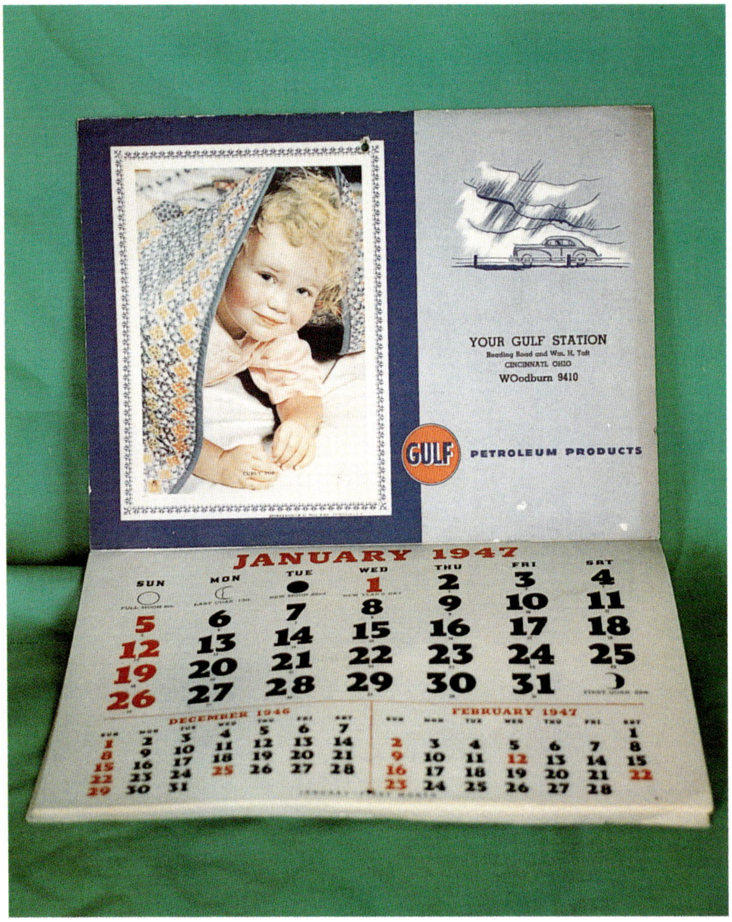


Calendar, value $25.

Calendar, 1982, value $20.

Libby Owens set of 4 glasses, value $20.

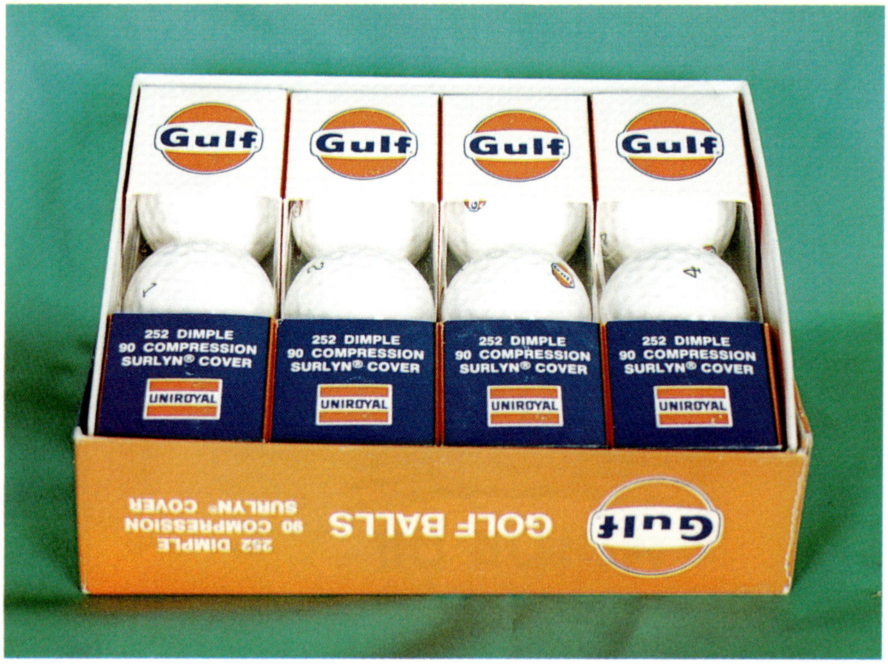


Dozen 1985 golf balls, sets of 3, numbered 1 through 4, value $100.

Whirlabout with string, value $25.

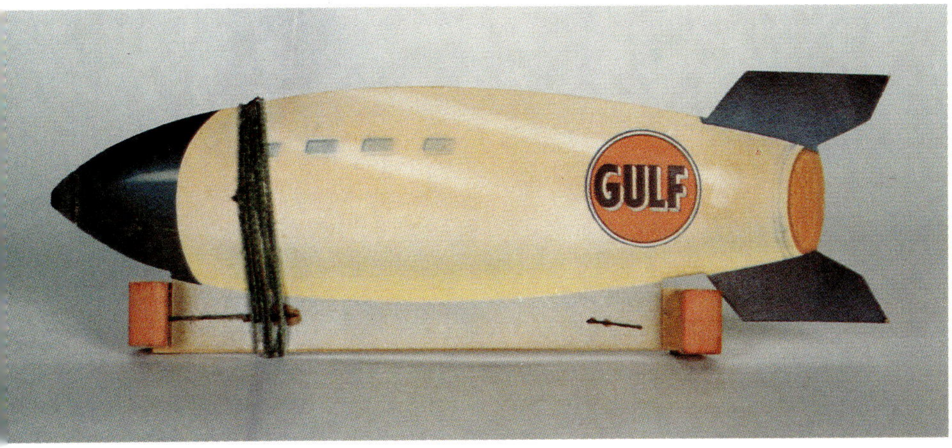


Blimp whirlabout with string, value $12.

Umbrella, 1987, value $30.

Worker hard hat, value $15.

Popgun, value $15.
Topcoat brush, value $10.
Bottom right, coat brush, 1930s $45.

1990s scratch pad, value $10.

Marbles, value $40 each. Crayons, value $15. Spinner top, $30. Golf marker, $20. Railroad car $10.

Fanny pouch, value $10.

1930s shoe-shine cloth, value not established.

Beach ball, value $20. License plate, value $12. Drinking glass, value $20.

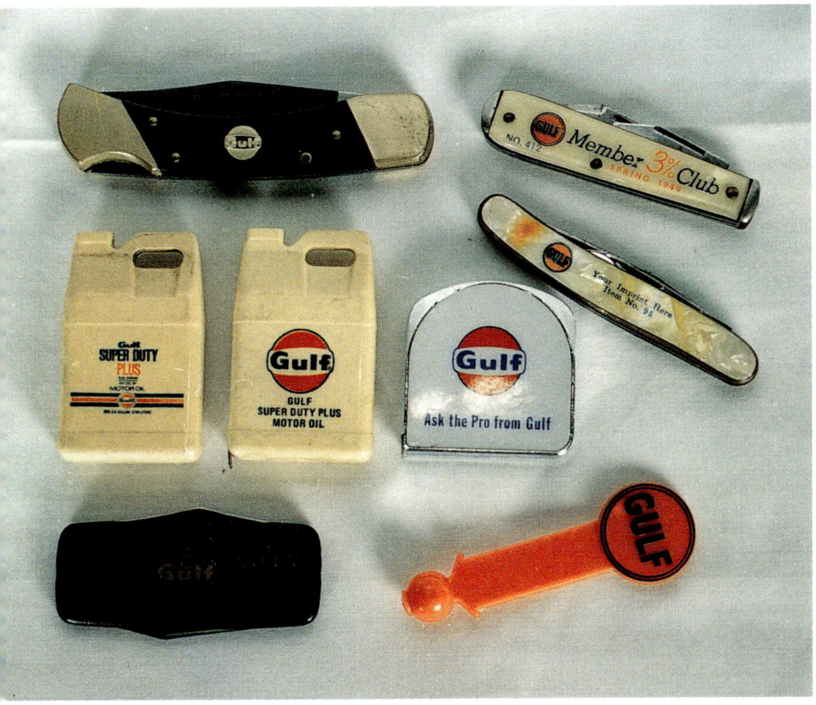


Pocket knives, value $12 to $20. Tape measurers, $15 to $20. Golf ball marker and divot repair tool, $20. Telephone dialing helper, value $5.

# Gulf Gear Lubricants

Quart, 1951, value $70.

Box and tube, 1951, value $50.

Left, 1951, value $40. Right, 1963, both 8 oz., value $25.

## Gulflube

1951, quart, metal, value $65.

1957 quart, metal, value $60.

1960 metal quart, value $60.

Five quart, 1948, value $90.

Quart, 1961, metal, value $70.

Five quart, value $75. Quart, metal, value $55.

Five quart, value $75. Quart metal, value $55.

Quart, metal, 1957, value $70.

Left, paper quart, value $12. Right, plastic quart, value $15.

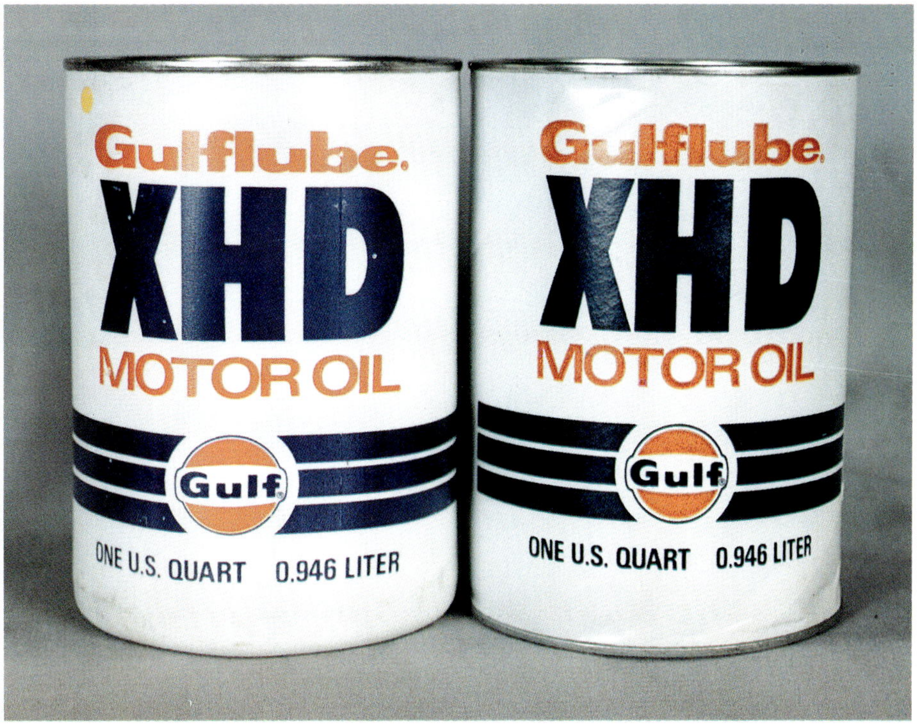


Left, 1984, plastic quart, value $12. Right, paper quart, 1984, value $12.

Heavy-duty truck oil, 1948-1950, value $55.

Left, 1988 plastic quart, value $12. Right, paper quart, value $10.

Paper, 1969, quart, value $25.

## Gulfmist

Display case with 12 cans, value $165.

Aerosol, 6 oz., value $10.

# Gulfoil Lubricants

Left, 1950s 4 oz. glass bottle, value $30. Right, 1930s 1.5 oz. glass bottle, value $80.

Metal, 4 oz., 1940s, value $40.

Metal, 1940s, 2 oz., value $40.

1940s metal, 4 oz., value $65.

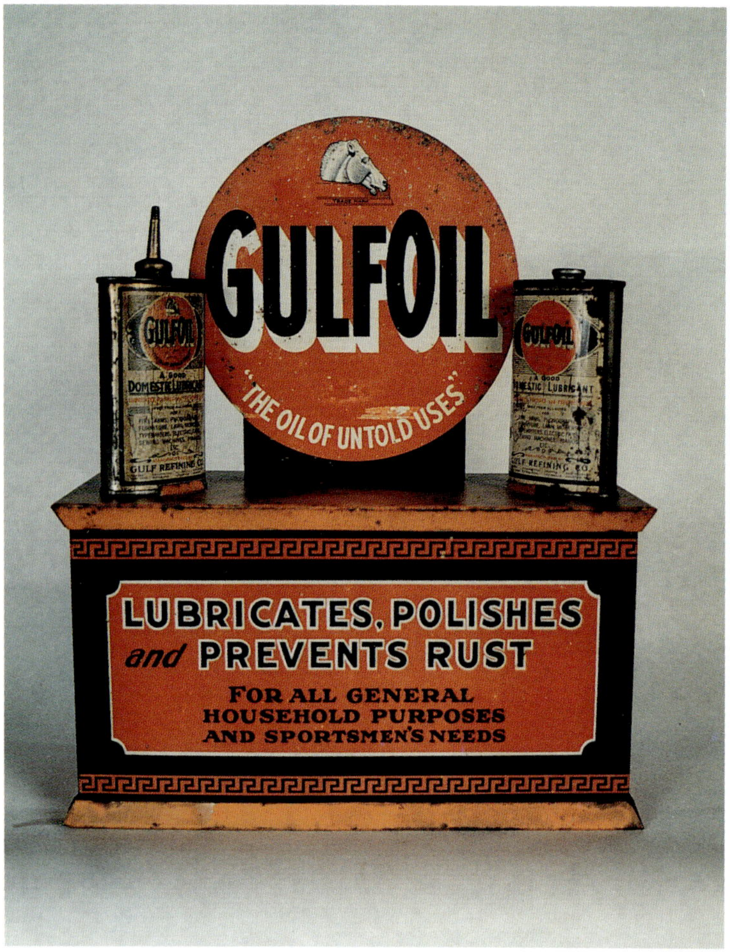


Display unit, 1940s, with containers, value $280.

Display unit only, 1930s, $165.

Various 4 oz. handy oilers shown left to right, 1960s, 1969, 1958, 1950, value $20 to $60 each.

# Gulfpride Motor Oil & Gulfpride Auto Diesel Oil

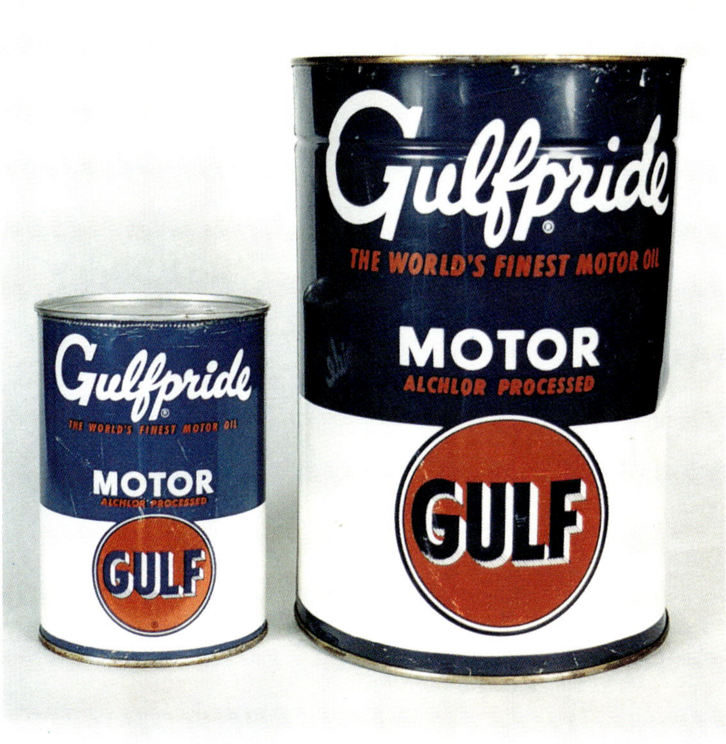


Quart, metal, 1951, value $30. Five quart metal, 1951, value $65.

Quart, early 1931, value not established.

Tall gallon, 1950s, value $60.

Tall gallon, value $65.

Quart, metal, 1942, value $65. Five quart, metal, 1942, value $95.

One gallon, 1920s to 1930s, metal, value $85.

Quart, metal, 1942, value $65. Five quart, metal, 1942, value $95.

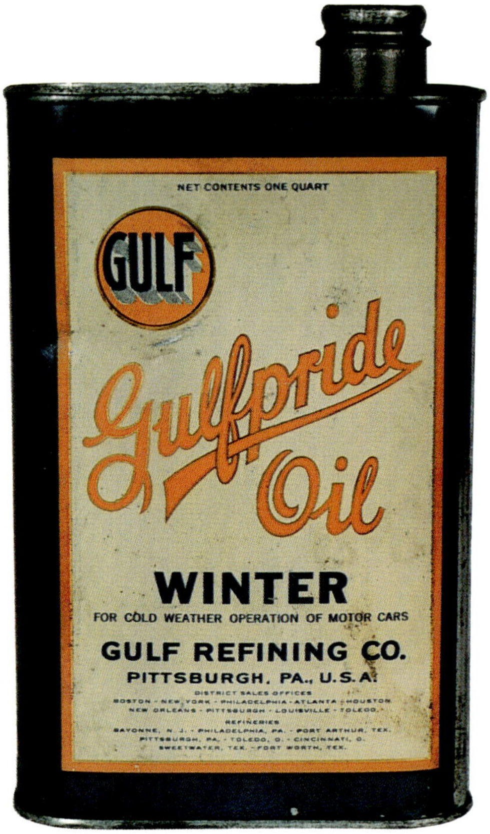


Quart, metal, 1920s to 1930s, value not established.

Glass quart with lid, 1942-1944, value $85.

Quart plastic, 1971, value $40.

Gallon, metal, 1968, value $65. Quart, paper, 1968, value $45.

Plastic promotional can, value $30.

Quart, paper, 1959, value $40. Quart, aluminum, 1959, value $40.

Paper, quart, 1984, value $15.

Quart, paper, 1971, value $60. Quart, plastic, 1968, value $40.

Quart, 1959, value $40. Five quart, metal, value $70.

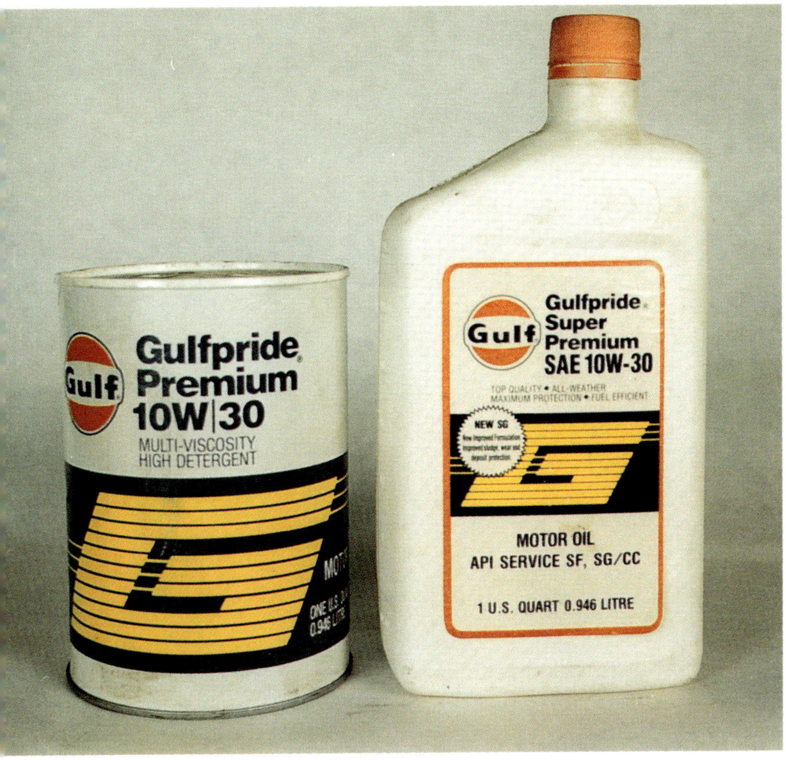


Paper, quart, 1984, value $15. Plastic, quart, 1984, value $15.

Plastic, quart, 1972, value $15.

Plastic, quarts, 1981, value $20 each.

# Gulfpride H.D. - Gulfpride H.D. Select - Gulfpride Select - Gulfpride Select Single-G

Metal, quart, 1951, value $45.

Quart, 1957, paper, value $45. Five quart, 1957, metal, value $75.

1957 promotional coin bank, value $25.

Metal, quart, 1951, value $45. Five quart, 1951, metal, value $70.

Metal, five quart, 1951, value $75. Metal, quart, 1951, value $50.

Metal, five quart, 1957, value $80. Metal, quart, 1957, value $55.

Metal, five quart, 1962, value $80. Metal, quart, 1962, value $50.

# Gulfpride Marine

Quart, metal, 1936, value not established.

Metal, one gallon, 1939, value $195.

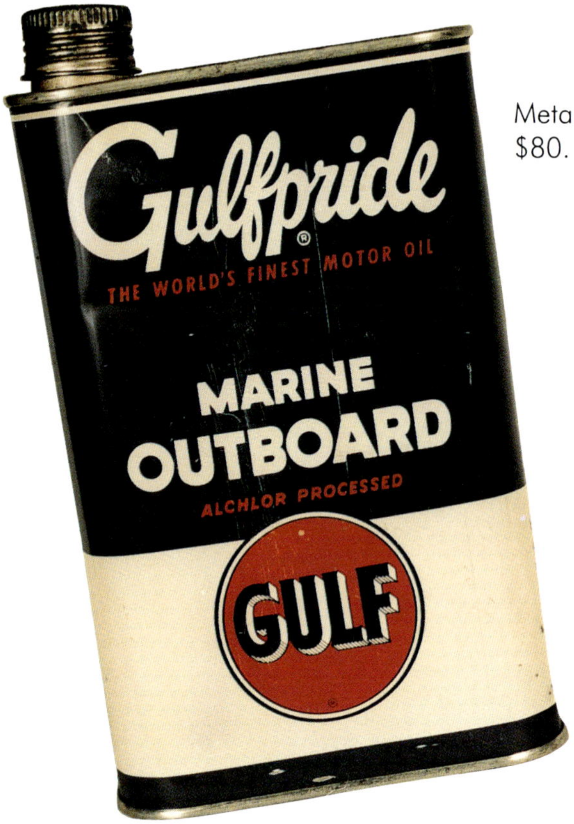


Metal, one quart, 1951, value $80.

Quart, metal, 1939, value not established.

## Gulfpride Marine G

Plastic, 1969, one quart, value $40.

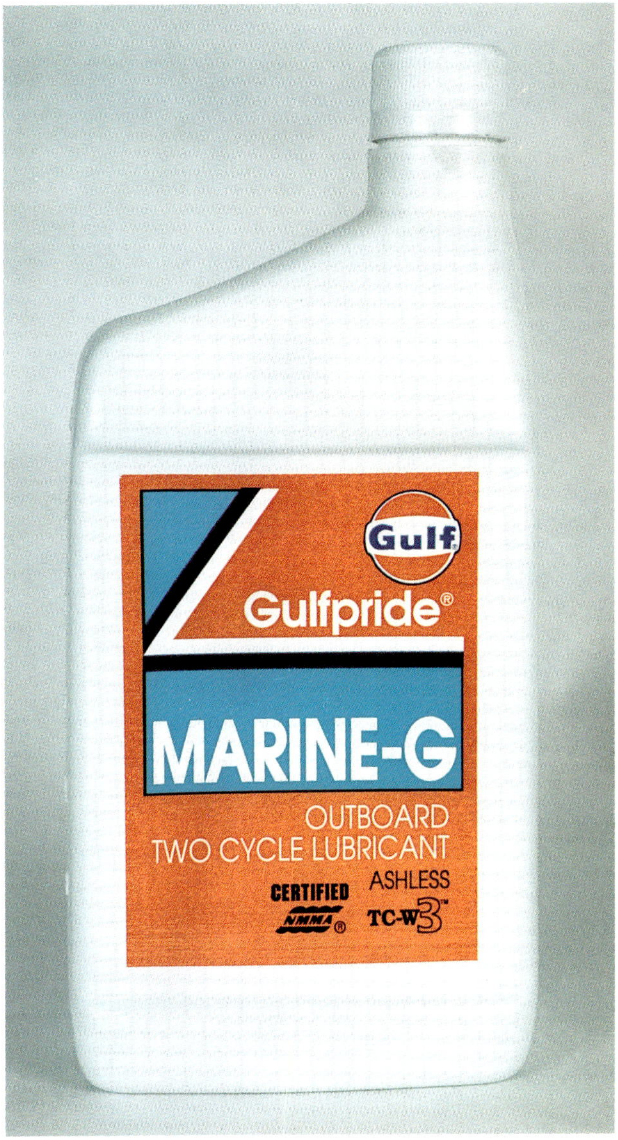


Plastic, one quart, value $35.

Pack of 3 with display carton, value $125.

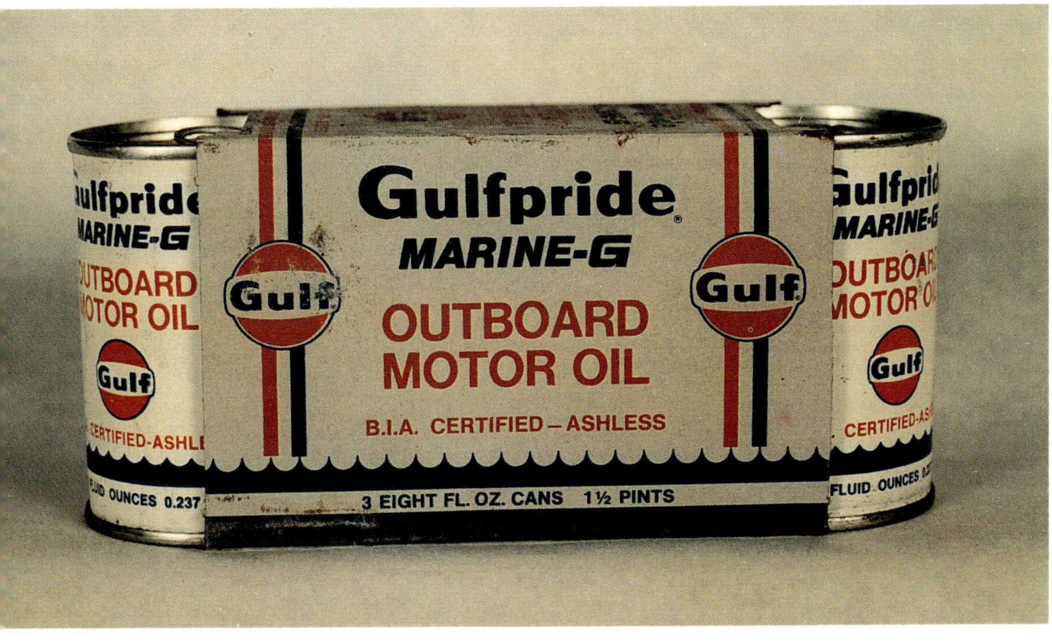

Single, metal, value $35.

Pack of 3 with display carton, value $125.

## Gulfpride Marine H.D.

Metal, one quart, value $125.

Metal, 1969, quart, value $100.

Plastic, 1975, quart, value $70.

# Gulfpride Multi-G

Paper quart, 1970, value $85. Metal gallon, 1970, value $80.

Paper quart, 1969, value $35. Metal gallon, 1970, value $65.

Quart, 1977, paper, value $15. Quart, plastic, value $20.

Promotional radio, 1977, value $40.

Quart, paper, 1977, value $30.

Pack of two in display, 8 oz., 1959, value $100.

## Gulfpride Outboard Motor Oil

Pack of three in display, 8 oz., 1959, value $130.

Plastic quart, 1963, value $50.

Plastic quart, 1980, value $40.

Metal, 1959, 8 oz., value $30.

Single, metal, 1964, 8 oz., value $35. Pack of 3 in display, 1964, 8 oz., value $130.

## Gulfpride Racing Oil

Left, paper quart, 1974, value $25. Right, paper quart, 1974, value $75.

Drinking glass, 1974, value not established. Self-sticking sticker, value $2.

Plastic quart, 1982, value not established.

Actual can used at LeMANS, 1974, value not established.

Picture of Steve McQueen, LeMANS, 1974, value not established.

# Gulfpride Single-G Oil

Paper, 1967, quart, value $35. Gallon, metal, 1967, value $80.

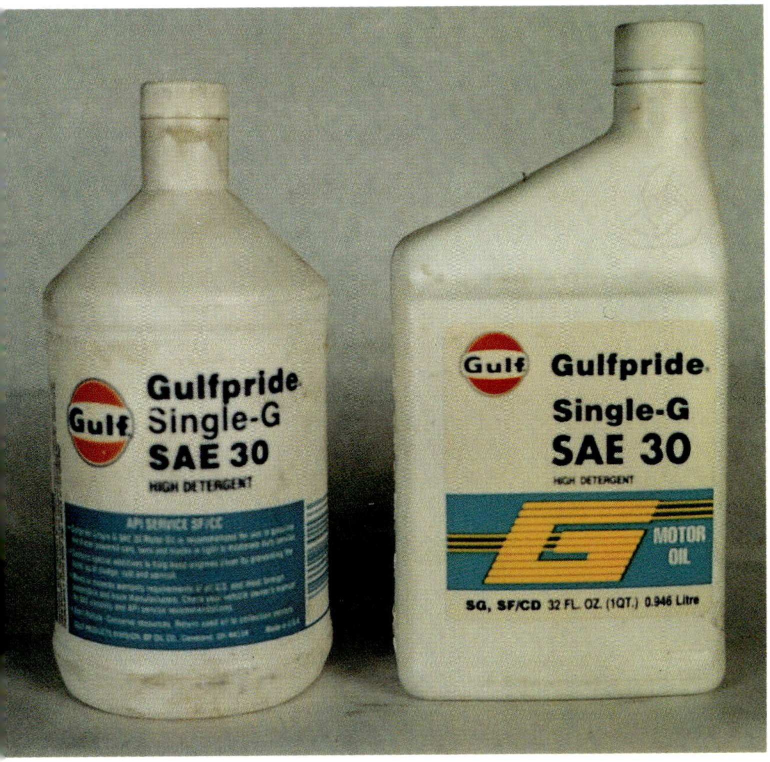


Left, plastic, 1984, quart, value $10. Right, plastic, 1984, value $10.

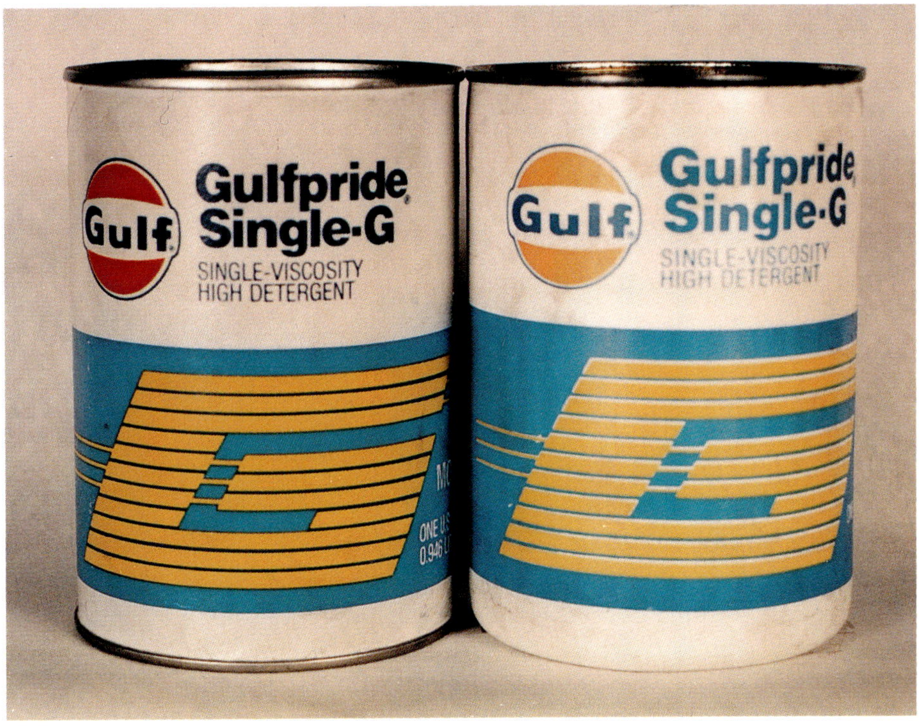


Left, paper, 1983, quart, value $10. Right, plastic, 1983, quart, value $30.

# Gulfpride Premium & Super Premium Oil

Left, plastic, 1984, quart, value $10. Right, paper, 1984, quart, value $5.

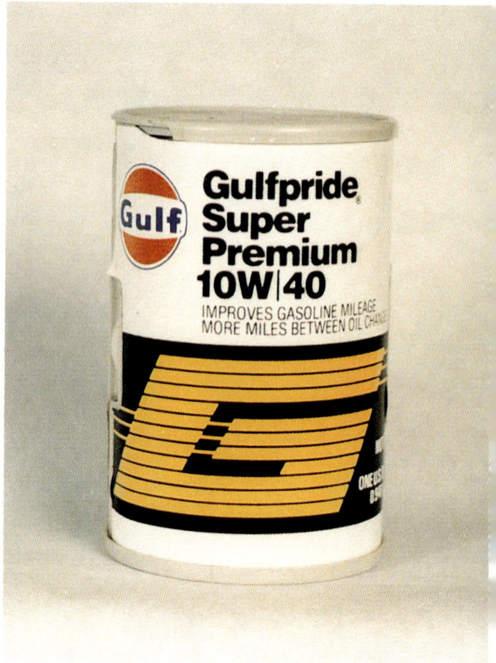


Promotional radio, 1984, value $40.

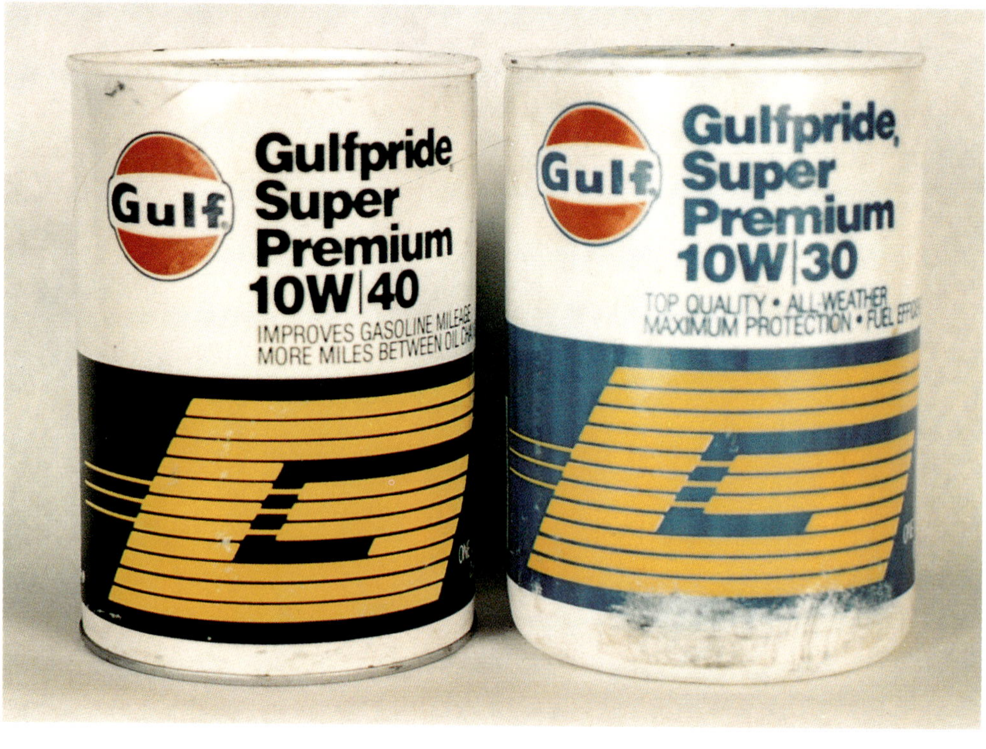


Left, paper, 1983, quart, value $5. Right, plastic, 1984, quart, value $10.

Left, quart paper; promotional radio, center; right, promotional golf balls in can, value $60 each.

Left, paper, quart, 1984, $5. Center, plastic, 1984, $10. Right, plastic, 1984, $10.

## Gulfpride Two Cycle Oil

Quart, 1994, value $10.

Quart, 1994, value $10.

## Gulfspray

Gallon, 1962, metal, value $30.

Metal, 6 oz. size, value $20.

Metal quart, value $30.

Quart, 1949, metal, value $30.

Glass quart, 1948, paper label, value $30.

Quart, metal, value $25.

Glass pint, paper label, 1947-48, value not established.

Quart, 1962, metal, value $25.

Quart, 1958, metal, value $35.

Aerosol, 1959, value $30.

Aerosol, 1964, value $35.

Pint, metal, 1954, value $15.

Quart, 1958, metal, value $15.

Quart, 1959, metal, value $30.

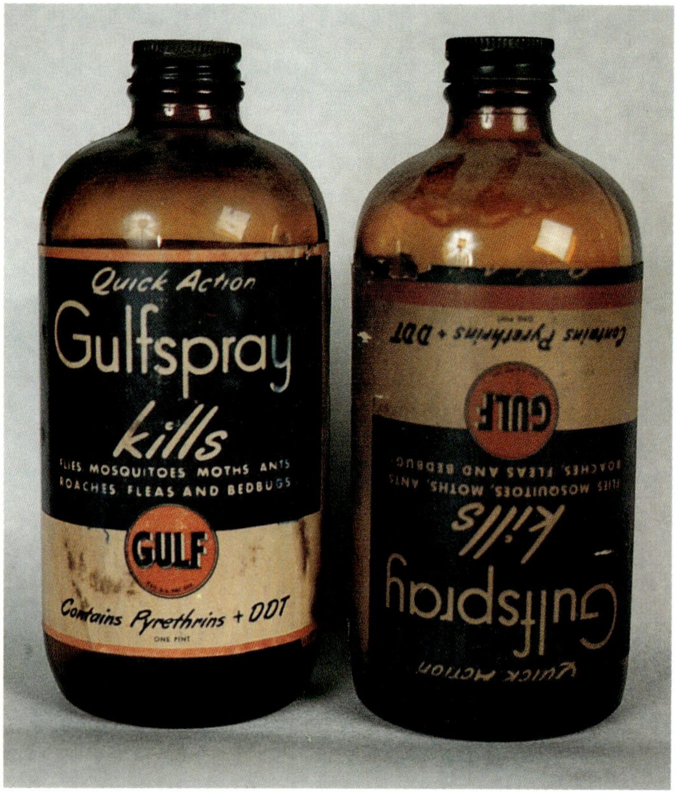


Glass pint containers, 1946, value $30 each.

Glass quart container, 1946, value $70.

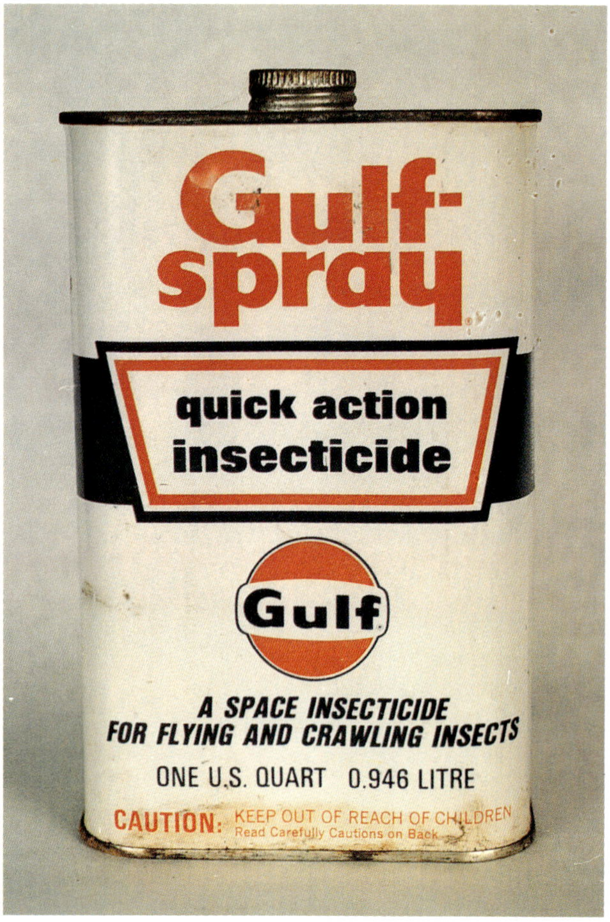


Pint, 1969, metal, value $20.

Quart, metal, 1969, value $30.

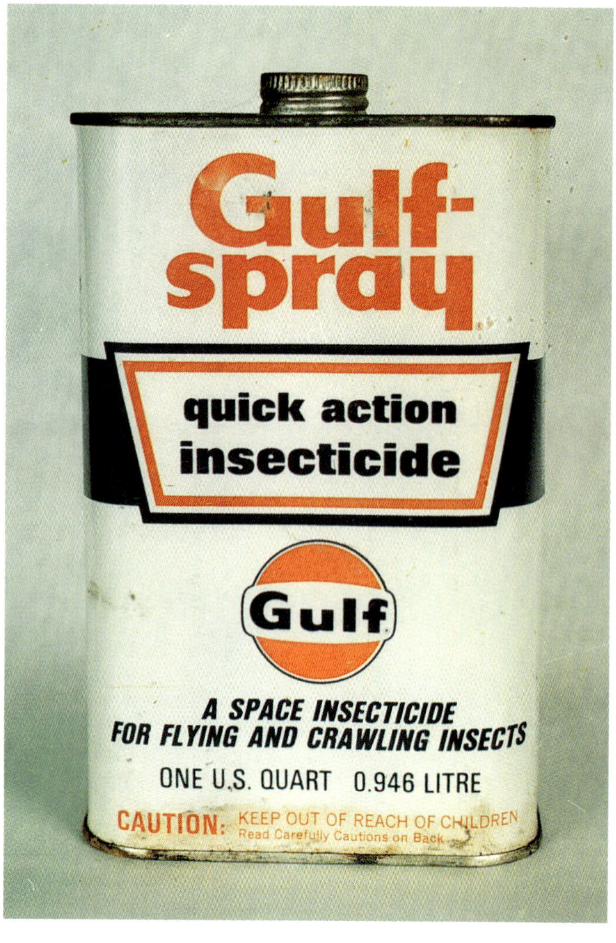

# Gulf Venom

Paper display, 1929, 3-D, complete, value not established.

1929 metal sprayer along with glass bottle of spray for sprayer, value not established.

# Gulflex

Plastic tube, 1958, value $20.

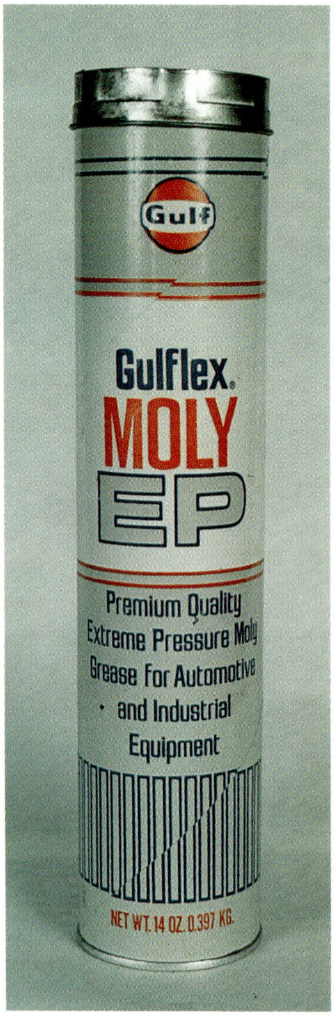


Paper cartridge, 1980, value $15.

One pound bearing grease, metal can, 1930s, value $25.

One pound waterproof grease, metal, can, 1930s, value $25.

One pound multi-purpose grease, 1953, value $25.

One pound metal can of joint lubricant, 1930s, value $25.

# High Pressure Grease

Cardboard carton for high-pressure grease tube, value not established.

Tube of high-pressure grease, 10 oz., shown with cardboard box container, value not established.

Metal 25-pound container, value $40.

One pound, metal, 1920s, value $55.

One pound high-pressure grease, 1930s, value $25.

Metal five pound container, early 1940s, value $60.

Metal five pound, round, value $25.

Metal five pound, 1948, value $50.

# Insect Repellants

Metal, 1975, 6 oz., spray, value $40.

Metal spray can, 1963, value $30.

Left, 1969; center, 1969; right, 1975, value $15 each.

# Kerolite Kerosene

Toboggan, 1982, value not established.

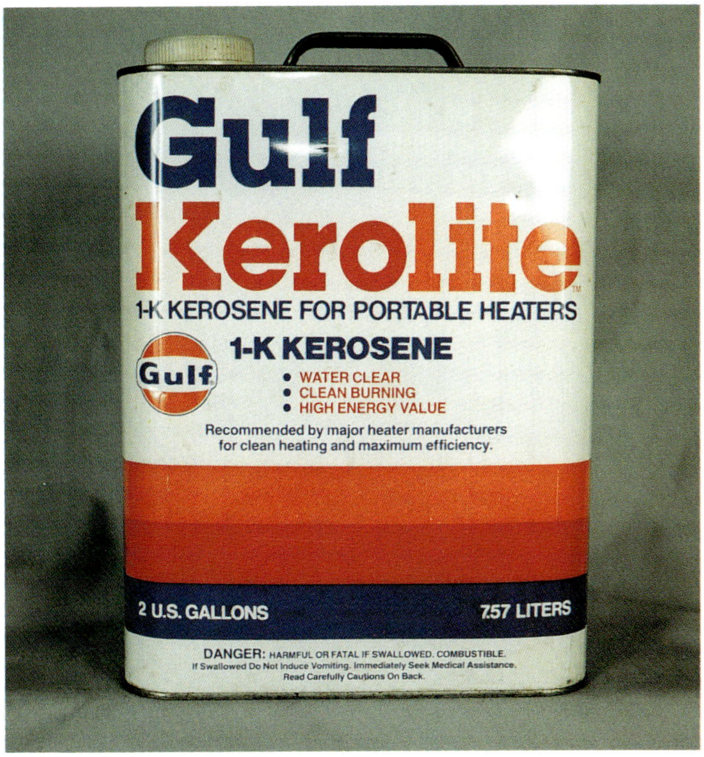


Metal two-gallon container, 1982, value $25.

Coffee cup, 1982, promotional item, value $25.

Two gallon, metal, 1982, value $45.

## Kleer Shield

Glass, 1953, gallon container, value $45.

Glass one gallon container, 1963, value $65.

Pint, paper wrapper, 1940s, value not established.

Plastic, quart, concentrate, 1963, value $45. Plastic applicator, $3.

---

## Lighter Fluid

Left, 1963, 10 oz., $10.
Right, 1963, 5 oz., $10.
Right, 1963, 5 oz., $20.
Right, 1958, 5 oz., value $45.

Left, 1954, 4 oz., value $50. Center, 2 oz., value $60. Right, 4 oz., value $30.

Glass containers, 4 oz., value $30 each.

---

## Livestock Spray & Sprayers

Glass one gallon container, value not established.

1940s one gallon metal can, value $40.

Sprayer, 1957 model, value $40.

Metal one gallon can, value $45.

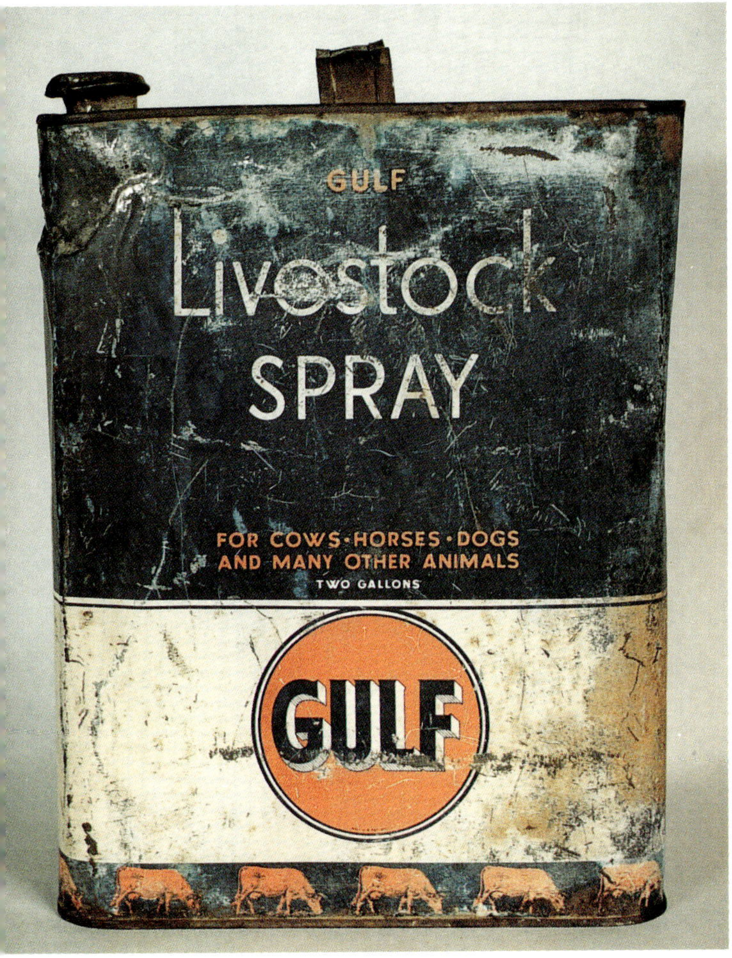


Metal two gallon can, value $50.

Quart metal can, value $70.

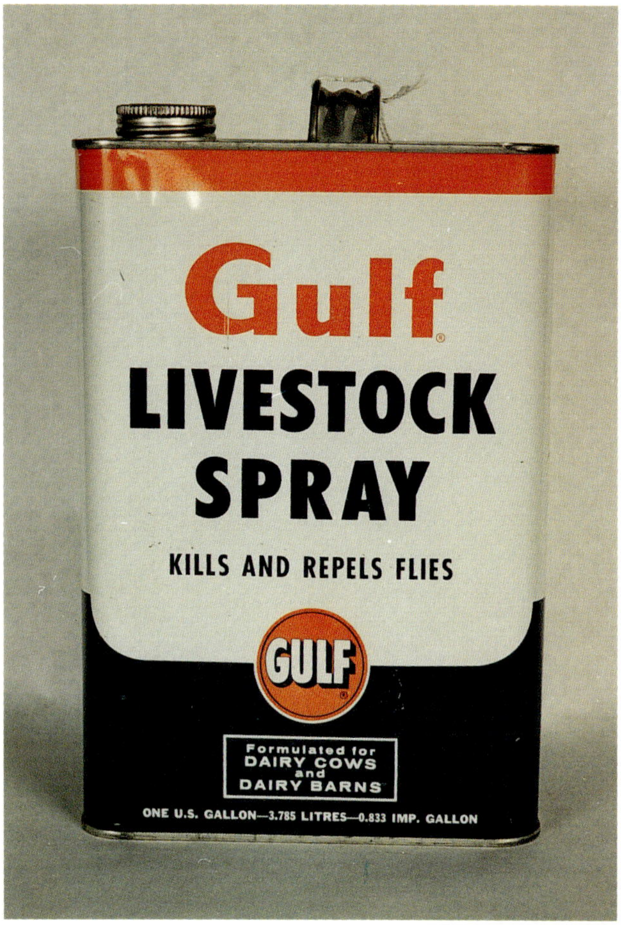


Gallon, metal, 1961, value $80.

Metal, 1964, one gallon, value $40.

## Lubricants and Silicones

One gallon, 1983, metal, value $40.

Metal, one gallon, 1953, value $80.

Left, 1964 spray, value $25. Right, spray, 1969, value $25.

Binder for 1964 *Dealer News*, value $300.

## Magazines/Books

June 1964 issue of *Gulf Dealer News*, value $10.

*Gulf Retail Sales Helps* magazine, value $30.

July-August 1934, *The Orange Disc* dealer magazine, value $8.

*Super Service* magazine, March 1949, value $12.

*Gulf News*, October 1943, value $12.

Display rack for *Disney Magazine*, value $20.

*Disney Magazine*, 1982, value $20.

*Gulf Service Station* magazine, value $20.

*Aviation Atlas*, 1948, value $20.

*Gulf Good Start Magazine*, 1960, value $15.

Hardbound book, early 1940s, on station dos and don'ts, value $200.

Two different brochures from 1951, value $20 each.

Uniform ordering brochure, 1960, value $15.

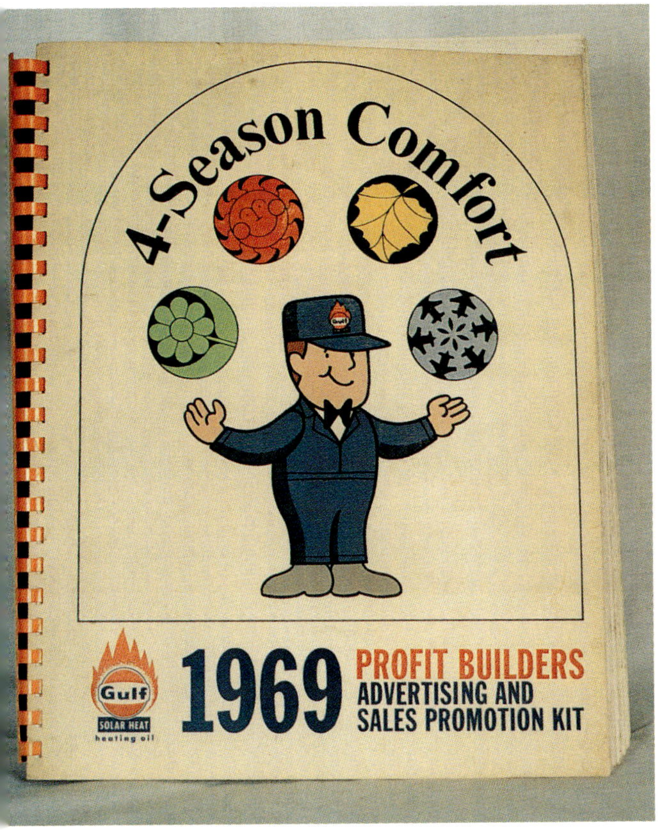


1969 promotional for solar heat oil, value $90.

Promotional brochure on lucky disc. Also shown are red, and white discs; disc $10 each, brochure $30.

Marine safety brochure with products displayed, value $20.

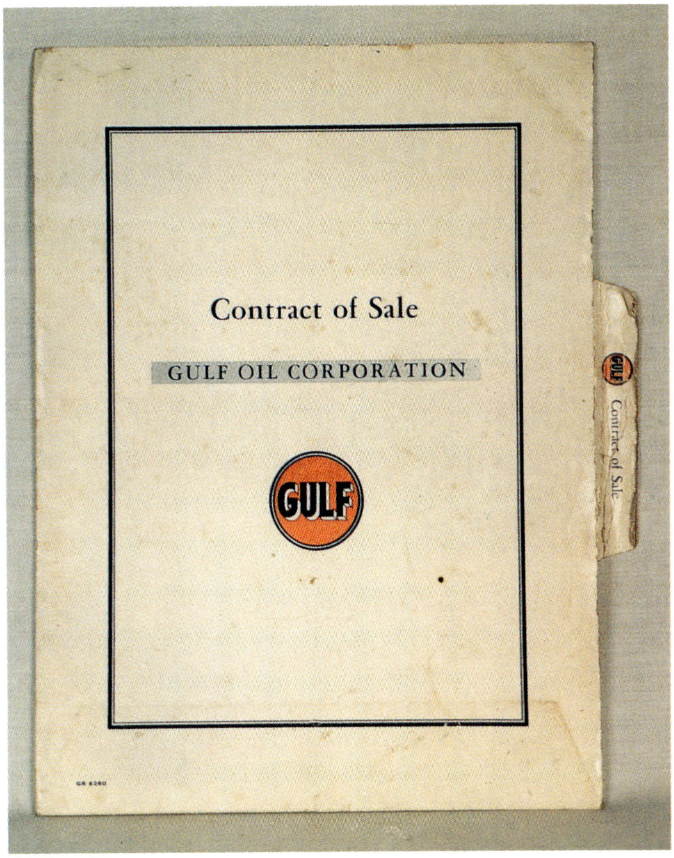


Service station Contract of Sale, various years. Shown here is 1956, value $30.

# Maps/Holders

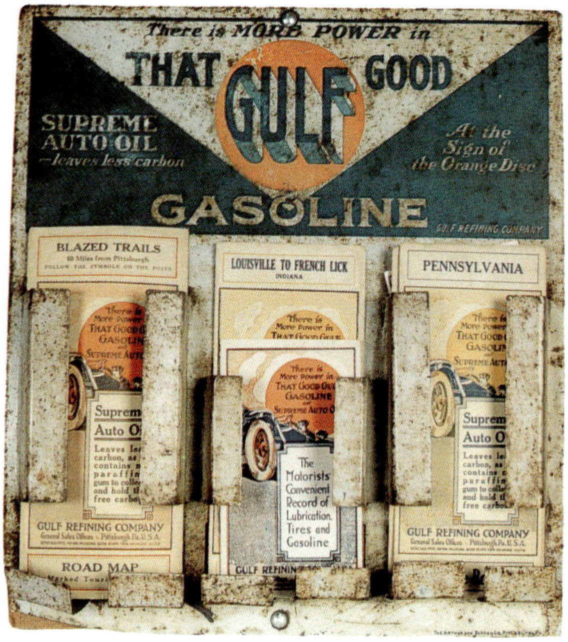


Two-wide by four-high holder, 1960s, value $150.

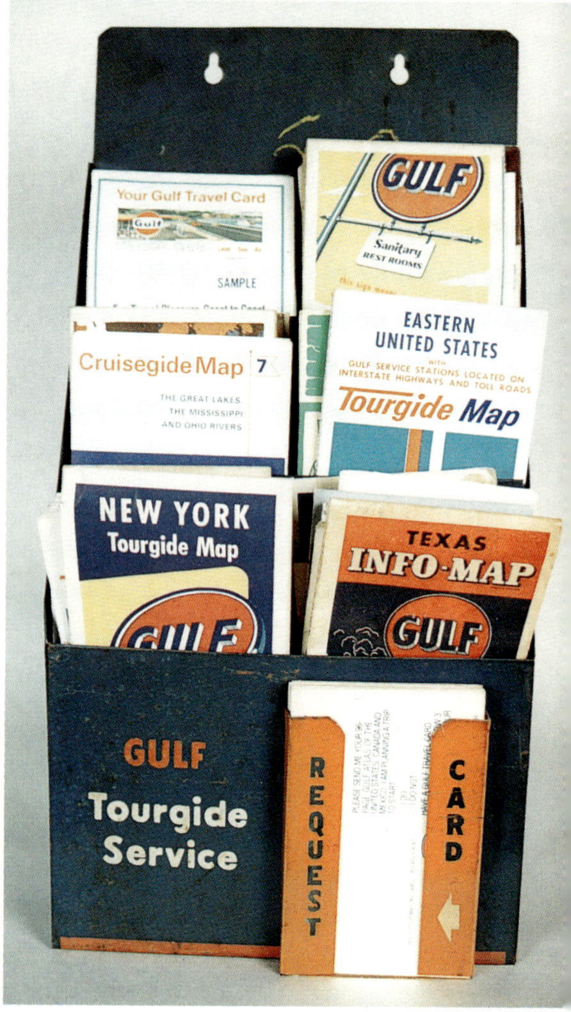


Holder, 1920s, value $200.

Two-wide by four-high holder, 1950s, value $175.

Four-wide by two-high holder, value $250.

# Miscellaneous Items

Bread wrapper from commissary in Port Arthur, Texas, value not established.

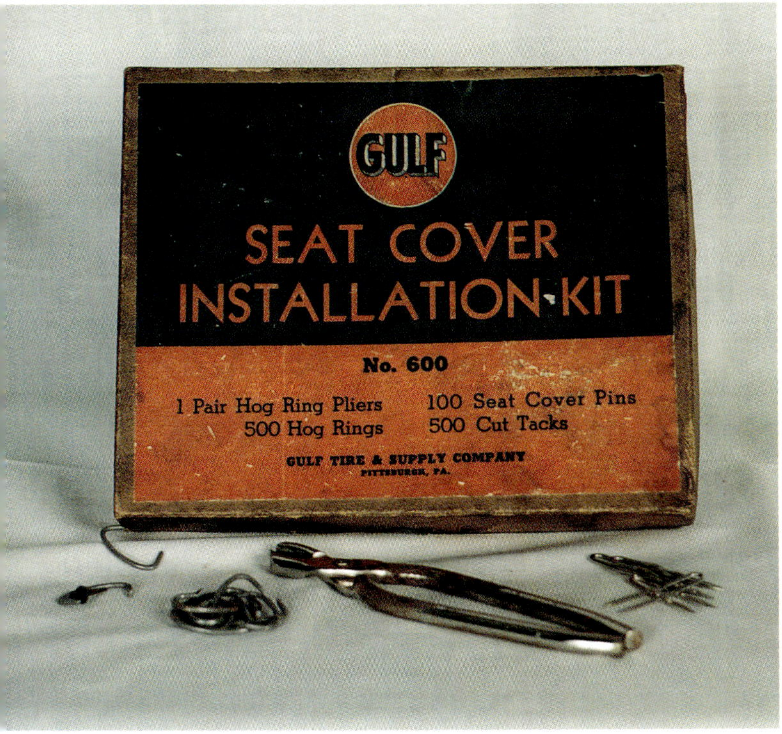


Seat cover installation kit, 1954, value not established.

Toy service station, 1950s design, value $250.

Red Top Grease, one pound and five pound sizes, values $15 and $5 respectively.

Indiana Gulf dealers promotional flyer and ring, value not established.

Paper label can of cleaning fluid one side, lighter fluid other, value $100 showing.

Various promotional items ranging from $30 to $100.

# Moth Proofers

Metal, 14 oz., 1961, value $35.

Metal, 14 oz., 1970, value $25.

Metal, 14 oz., 1958, value $50.

Paper bag with hanger for storage of coats, 1963, value $100.

Metal, 14 oz., 1965, value $40.

Metal, can, 14 oz., 1955, value $50.

## No Nox

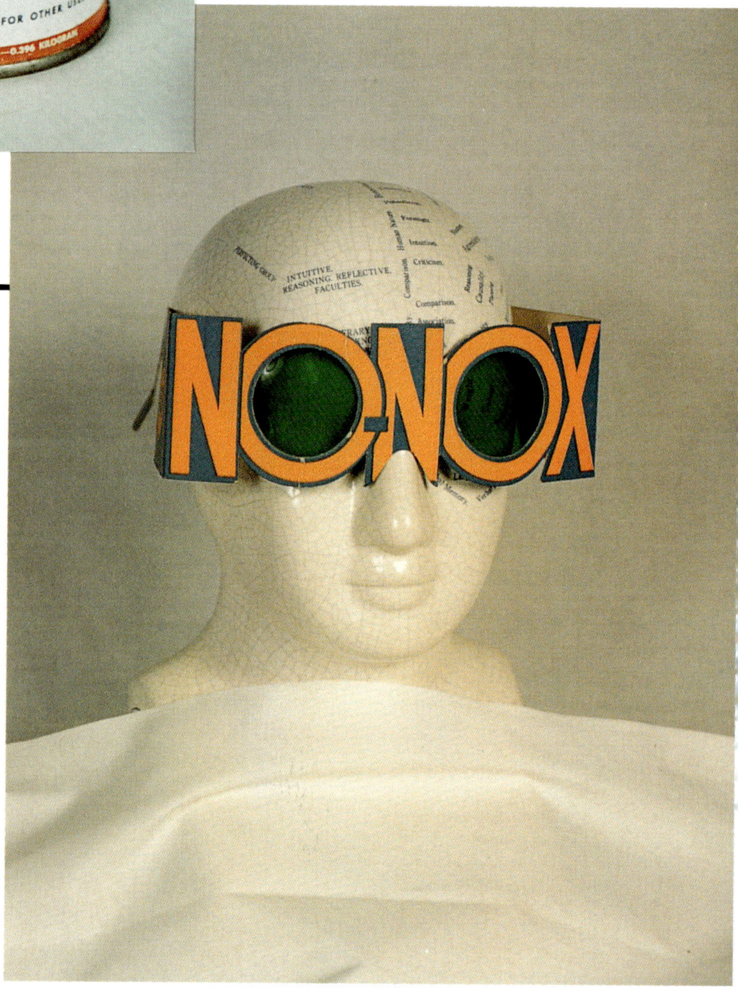


Cardboard sunglasses, value not established.

## Orchard Spray

One gallon brown glass, bottle value not established.

## Paint

Black tire paint, value $20.

Aerosol, 12 oz., gray paint, value not established.

## P.A.C.

Metal, 1952, value $15.

Metal, 1966, value $10.

# Part Ease - Dripless Oil - Lock Ease

Metal, 12 oz., 1964, value $15.

Metal, 4 oz., 1964, value $15.

Metal, 4 oz., 1964, value $15.

---

# Pencils/Pens

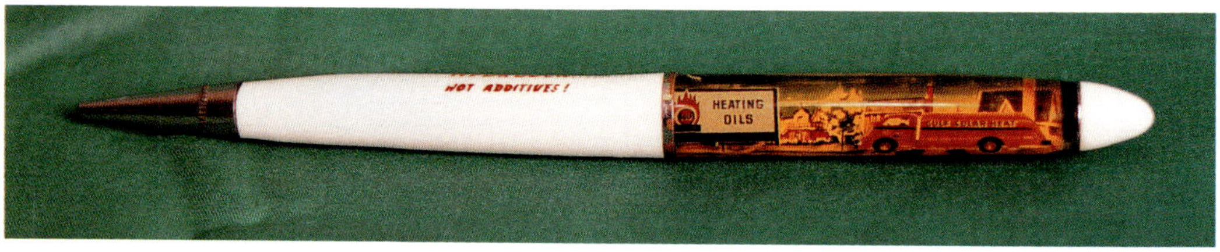


Gulf Solar Heat truck suspended in fluid, value not established.

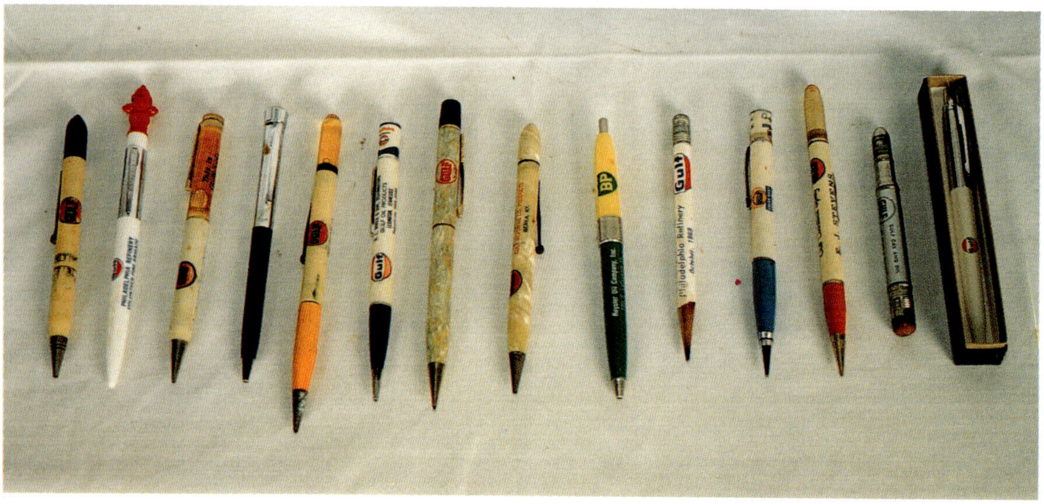

Pencils and pens from $12 to $35.

# Penetrating Oil

Metal, gallon, 1942, value $30.

Metal, 2 oz., lead spout, value $45.

Metal can, paper label, 1920s, value $65.

Metal, half pint, 1940s, value $45.

Metal, 4 oz., 1940s, value $25.

Glass 4 oz. bottle, 1930s, value $35.

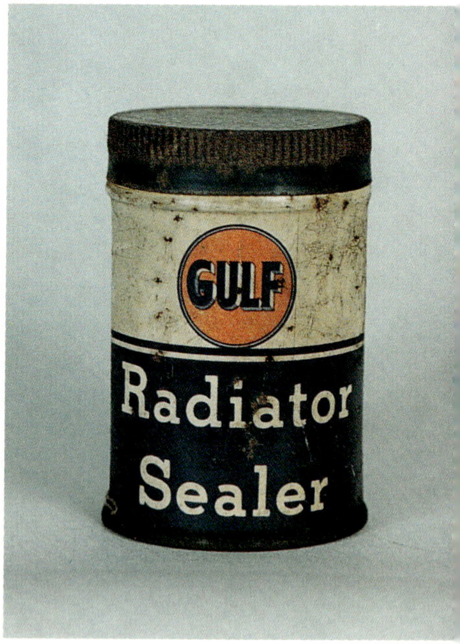


Metal, 1953, 2 oz., value $25.

## Radiator Hose - Radiator Sealer - Gasket Cement - Rim Cement

Gasket cement in glass bottle, 1953, value $35.

Rim cement, paper label, value $55.

Hose, 1971, value $2.

## Rain Gauges

Value $10.

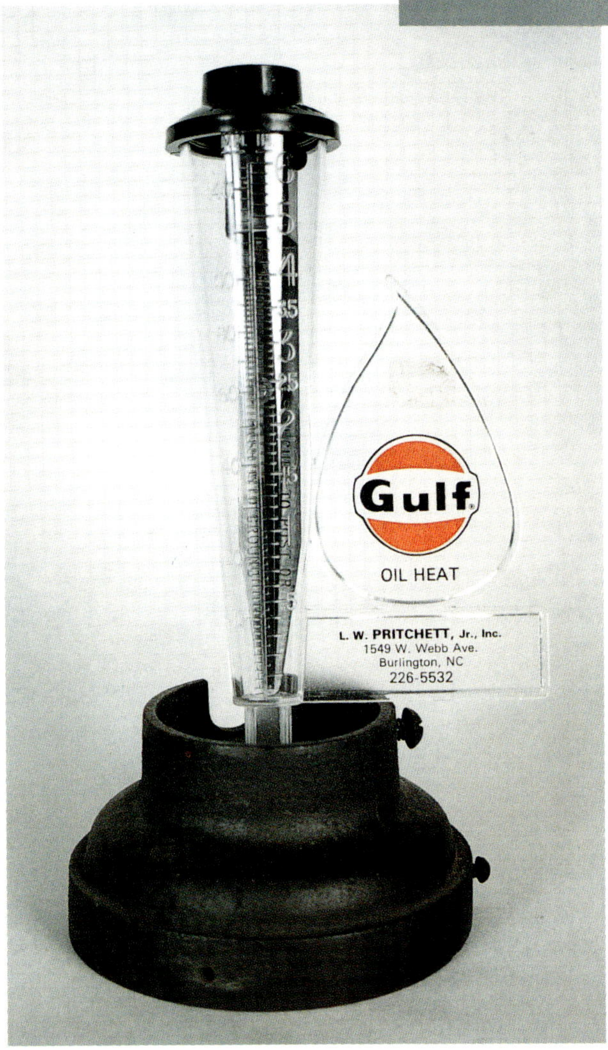


Value $10.

## Restroom Signs - Locks - Tags

Plastic key holders, left, 1983, value $40 for set. Gulf padlock, value $90. Sign "Locked," value $65. Tags, left, 1984, set of 2, value $45. Tags right, set of 2, value $80.

---

## Roach & Ant Killer

Metal pint, 1948, value $25.

Metal spray can, 1961, value $45.

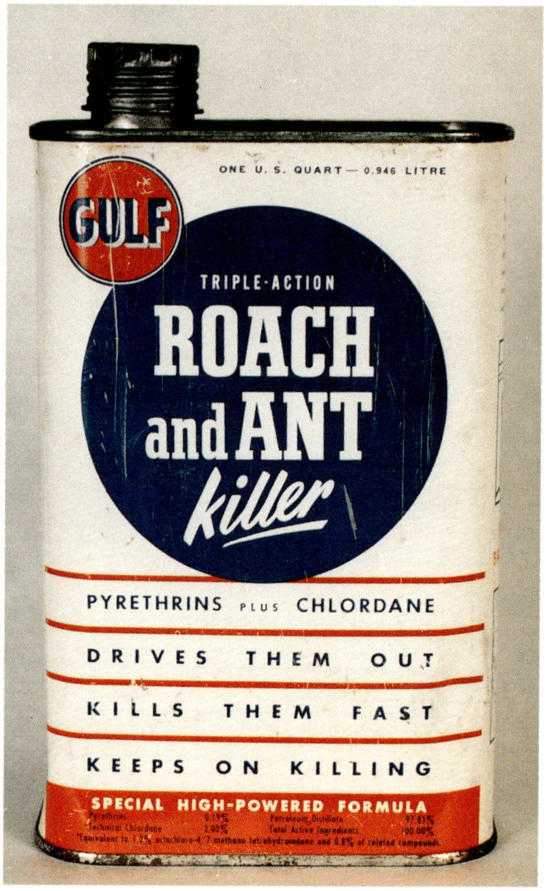


Metal quart, 1953, value $55.

# Salesmans Oil Sample Breakdown Kits

Display case showing various grades of oil from raw product, value $250.

Display showing various grades of oil and greases from raw product, value $250.

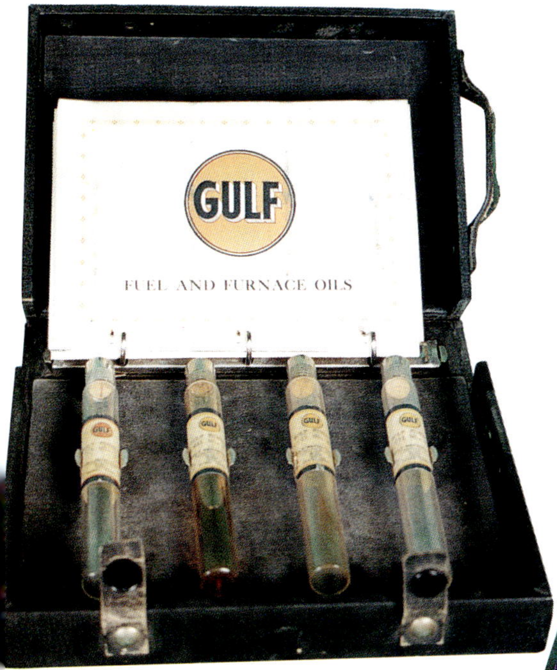


Display of solar heat grades of fuel available, value $175.

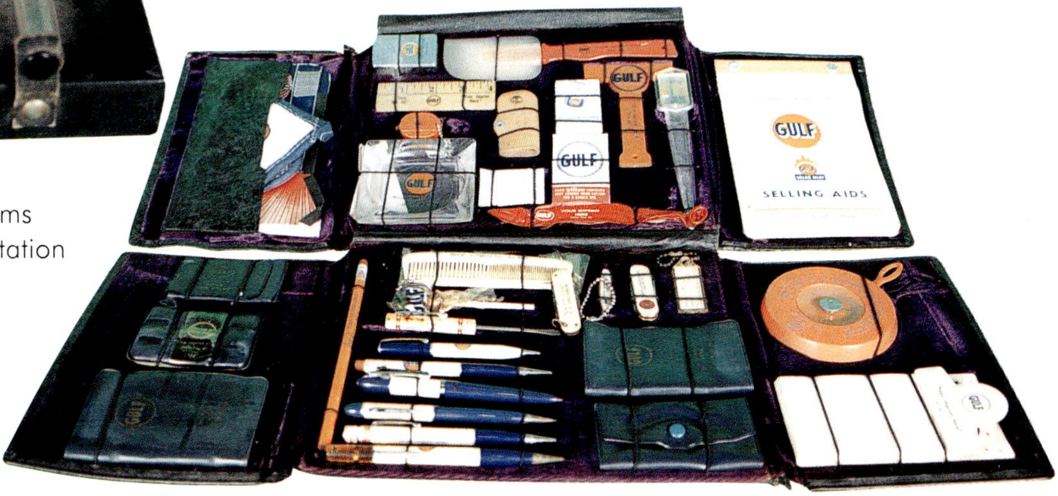


Display of promotional items available to Gulf service station dealers, value $450.

# Salt & Pepper Shaker Sets

Lunch pail type, value $45.

Pair of orange, value $175.

Pair as shown, value $135.

# Saphire Supreme Motor Oil

1962 paper, quart, value $45.

1966 paper, quart, value $30.

Left, paper, 1977, value $20. Right, paper, 1977, value $20.

Gallon, 1962 version, value $70.

Gallon, metal, 1977, value $20.

Gallon, metal, 1963, value $20.

## Seasonal Fuel Conditioner - SDL

Metal, cone top, 1958, value $25.

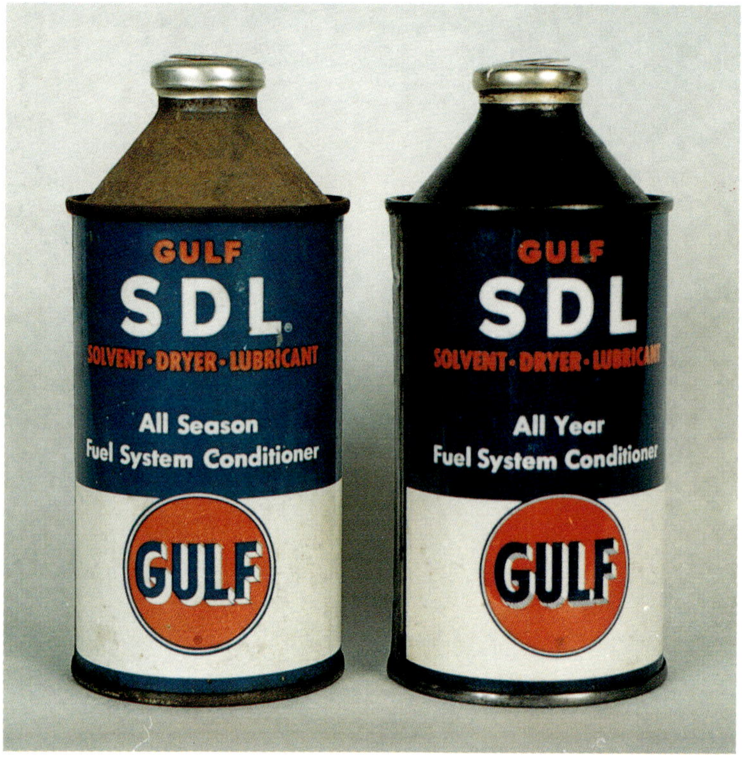


Metal, cone top, 1958, two versions of printed can, value $25 each.

---

## Shocks

Gulf display box with shock, 1983, value $20.

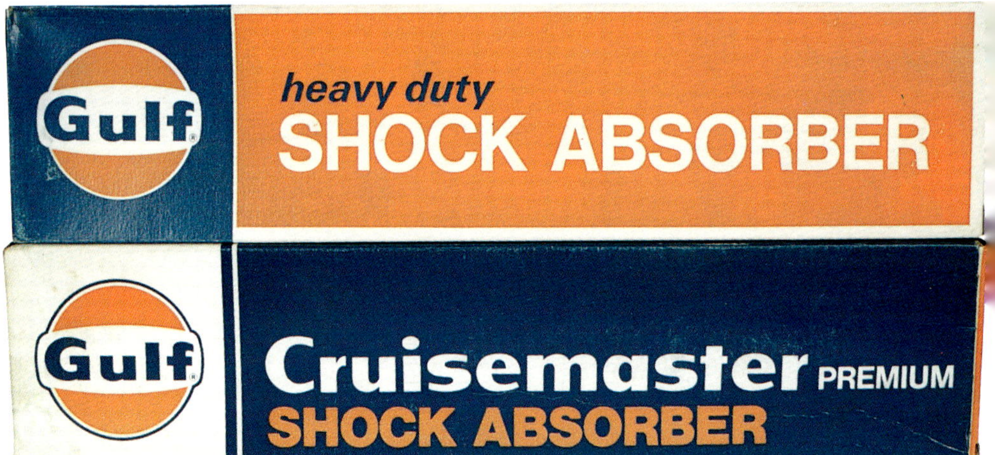


Two shocks, both 1983, value $20 each.

## Signs - Displays

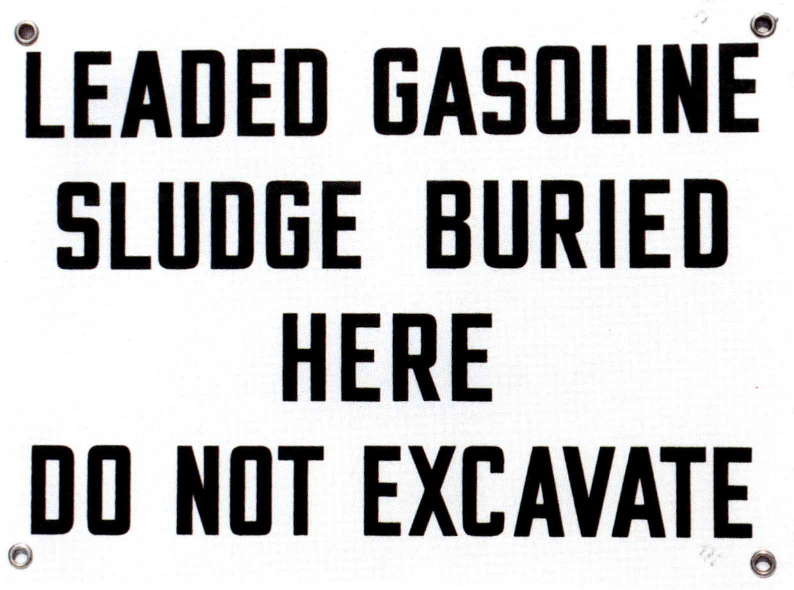


Porcelain metal sign, value not established.

Cast iron station pricing plate, value not established.
*Courtesy of L Herbermann.*

Pump plates both for same pump for gas and oils, left, value $100; right, value not established.

Lighted sign, value $100.

Desk lamp, value $45.

Plaque, 1986, new beginning, value not established.

Brass spittoon with the word Gulf embossed in metal, value not established.

Tire branding iron for branding Gulf tires on company vehicles, value not established.

Service station work order card holder, value $150.

Gulf tire, $70. Advertising insert, $15. Tire stand holder, $20.

Well pump sign, value $125.

Display for Gulf products, cardboard, value $50.

Lighted desk display, value $120.

Gulf well pump sign, value $150.

Pump plate sign, value $100.

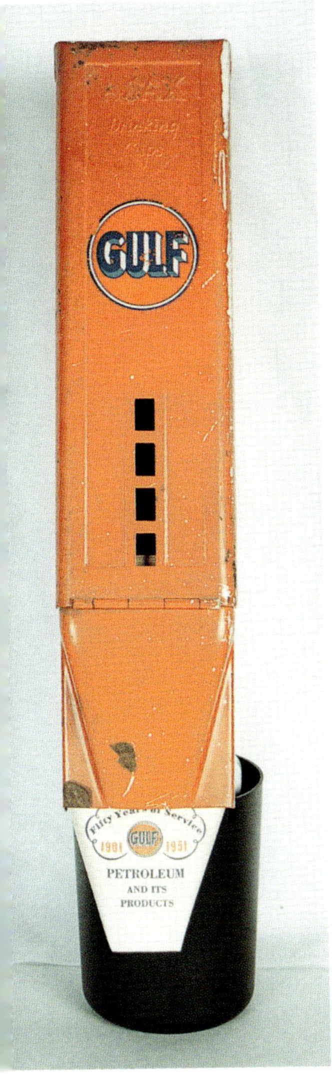


Service station drinking cup dispenser with cup, value $175.

Lighted display sign, value $175.

Station banners, value not established.

Lighted 18-inch sign, value $100.

Pump plate, value $125.

Gas pump plate, set of two, value $150.

Display with products, 1983, value $75.

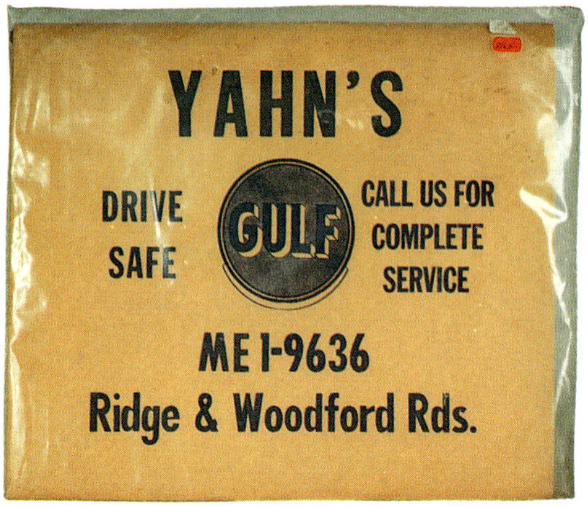


Stadium seat cushion, Cincinnati, Ohio, area schools, value $40.

1964 display with tools, value $125.

Pricing sign, value $60.

---

## Sprayers

Livestock sprayer, electric, quart size, value $100.

Collection of Gulf space sprayers, value $12 to $20.

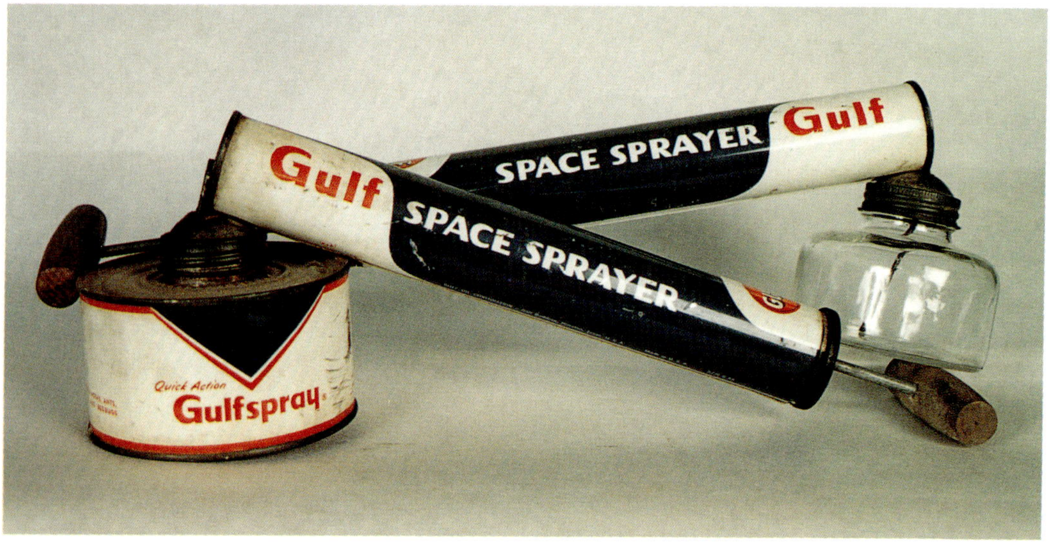


Collection of space sprayers, value $10 to $20.

## Staplers

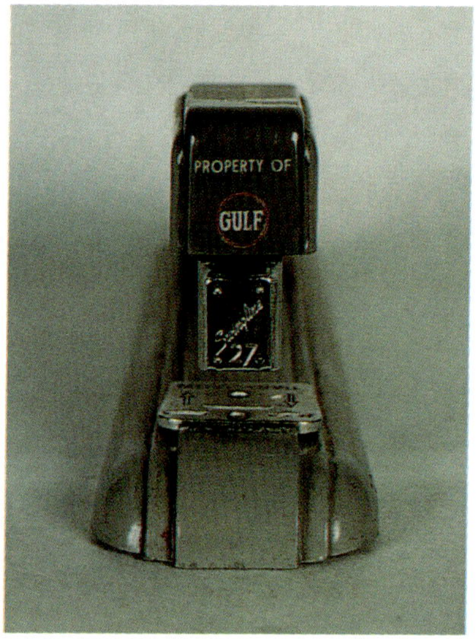


Desk stapler, value $25.

## Tank Markers

Driveway marker for gasoline underground tanks, value not established.

Driveway markers to indicate grade of products for gasoline underground tanks, value $10 each.

## Super Duty Motor Oil

Paper, quart, 1983, value $25.

Gallon, plastic, 1981, value $25.

Left, plastic quart, 1975, value $20. Right, paper quart, 1970, value $40.

Paper quart, 1962, value $45.

Left, paper, quart, 1971, value $20. Right, paper, quart, 1963, value $30.

## Super G Synthetic Motor Oil

Left, plastic quart; right, metal quart, values not established.

## Supreme Products

Gallon, 1920s, value $100.

Pail, five pounds, value $75.

One gallon, 1920s, value $75.

Five pound container, 1940s, value $50.

Pail, five pounds, 1920s, value $75.

One pound, 1920s, value $90.

One gallon, 1920s, metal, value $75.

One-pound versions, 1940s, value $80 each.

Left, 1960, metal quart, value $75. Right, metal quart, 1957, value $100.

Two gallon, 1960, value $40.

Two gallon, 1957, value $50.

Left, metal quart, value not established. Right, metal quart, value not established.

## Telephone

Telephone and box for Gulf phone, value $60.

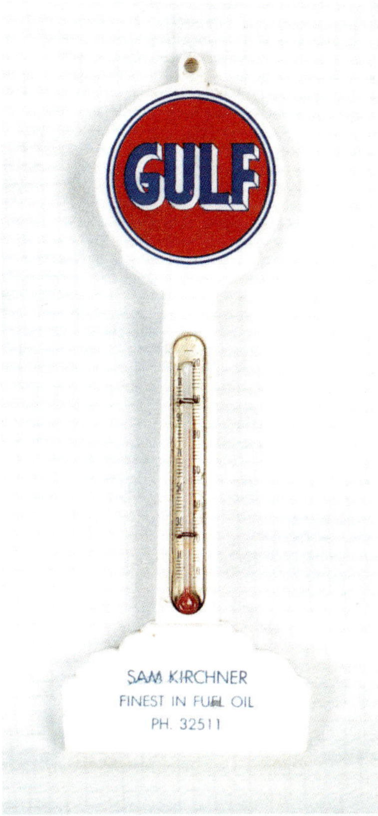


Thermometer sign, pole type, value $40.

## Thermometers

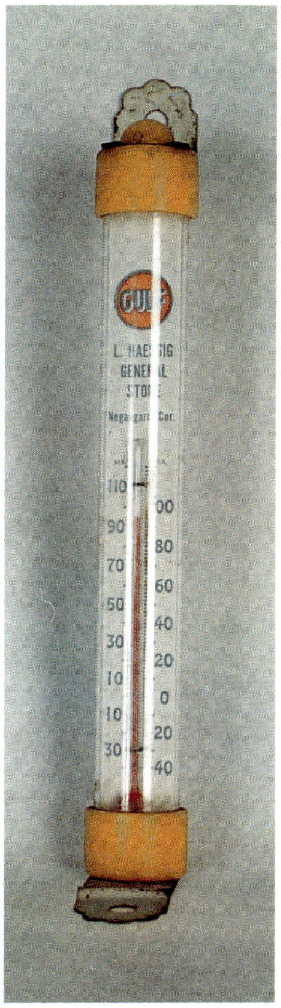

Outdoor window-ledge type, value $25.

Outdoor oval thermometer, value $100.

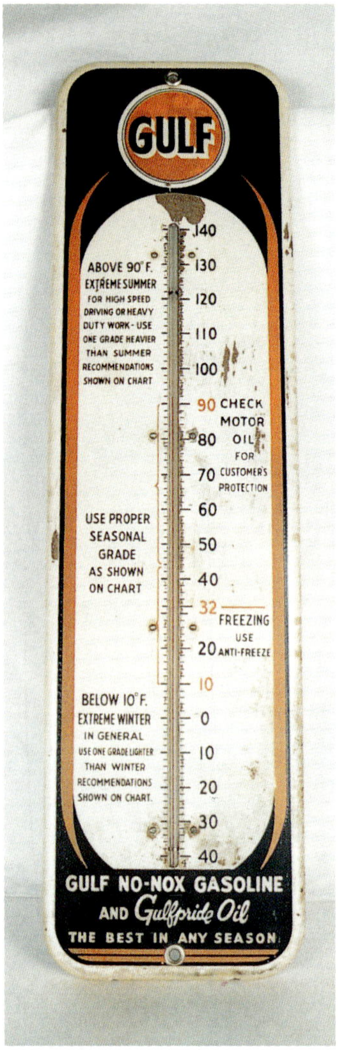


Outdoor, 1950s, value $190.

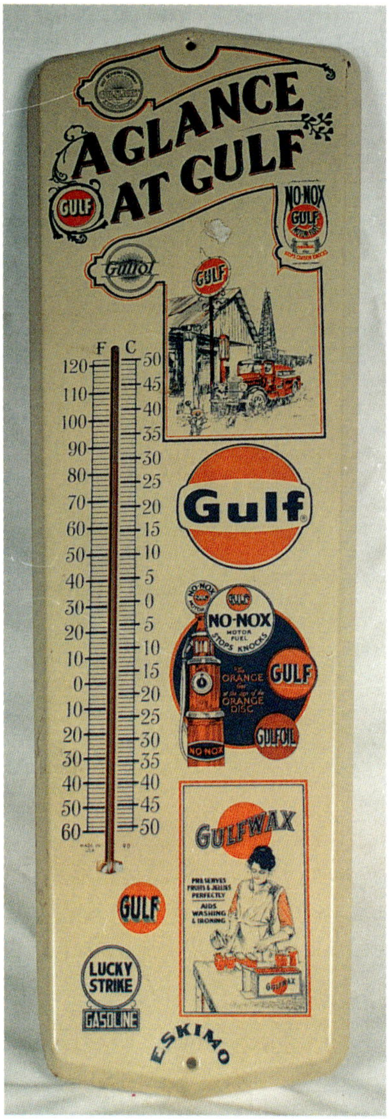


Outdoor, 1986, value $90.

# Tie Clasp & Tie

Gulf tie, value $25. Tie clasps, value $15 to $20.

## Torch Fuel

Metal, 1971, value $60.

## Tour Guide

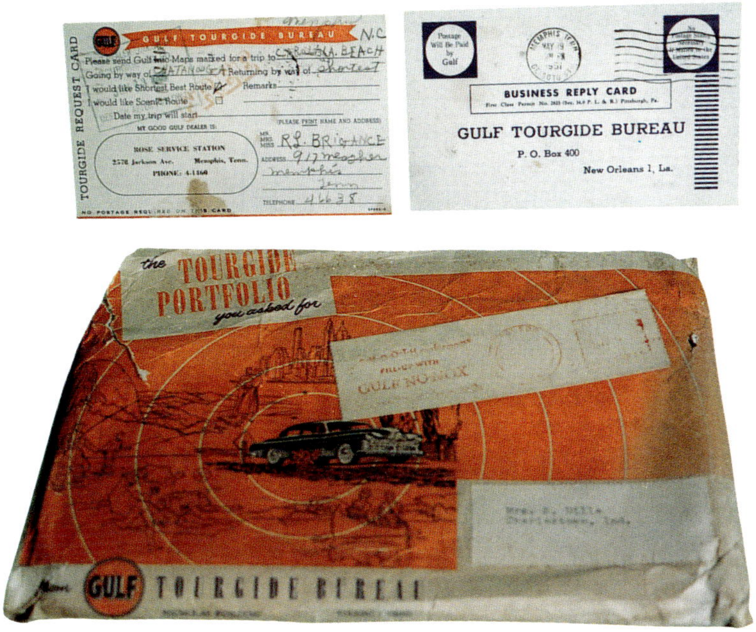


Tour package with maps and tourguide postcards for next trip, value $20.

Information log books contained in tour map packages, value $20 for all three items.

## Towels

Towels, value $30 each.

## Traffic Motor Oil

Gallon, metal, 1930s, value $100.

## Tractor Fuel

Tractor Fuel tag for containers of tractor fuel, value $25.

# Trak and Tag

Gallon, metal, 1951, value $80.

Left, pint, 1951, metal, value $45. Right, quart, metal, 1949, value $50.

Spray bomb, 12 oz., 1954, value $40.

Various space sprayers, value $45 to $75.

Left, pint, 1940s glass bottles, $40. Center, Tag, $75. Right, Tag, $85.

Quart, 1940s glass bottle, value $40.

## Transmission Lubricants

One gallon, 1920s, value $75.

Five-gallon screw cap container, 1920s, value $80.

## Tri-AD

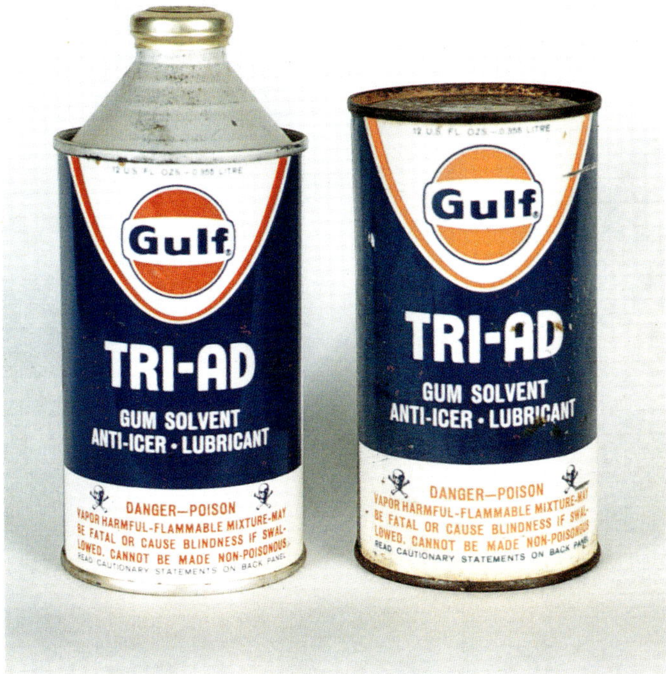


Metal, 12 oz., both 1963, value $12 each.

## Trucks Toy

Gulf delivery trucks, value $60 each.

# Tube Patches, Seals, & Tubes

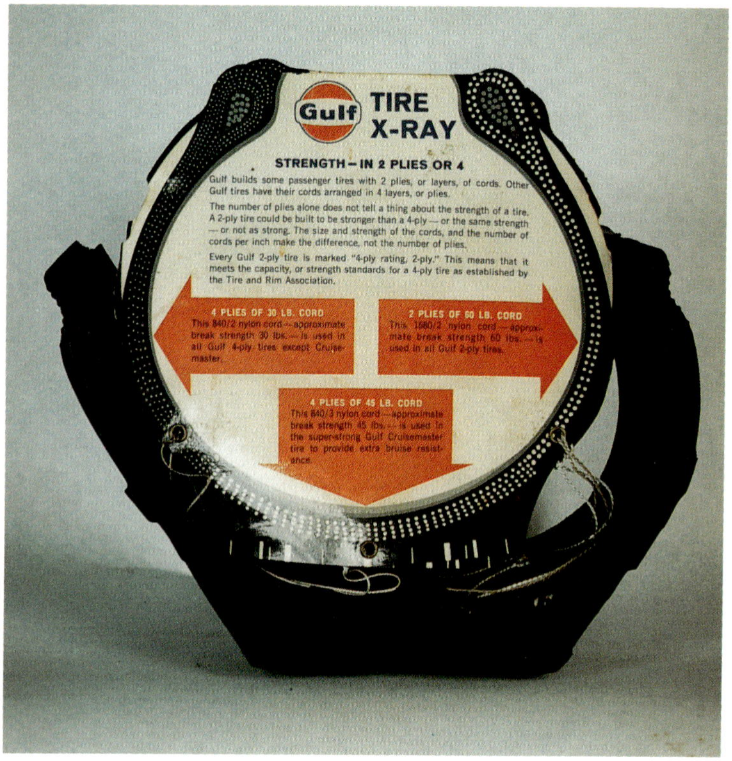


Cut-away section of Gulf tire with display advertising, value not established.

Tire vulcanizing cement, paper label, 1954, value not established.

Tube patches, 1954, value not established.

Tube and box, 1954, value $35.

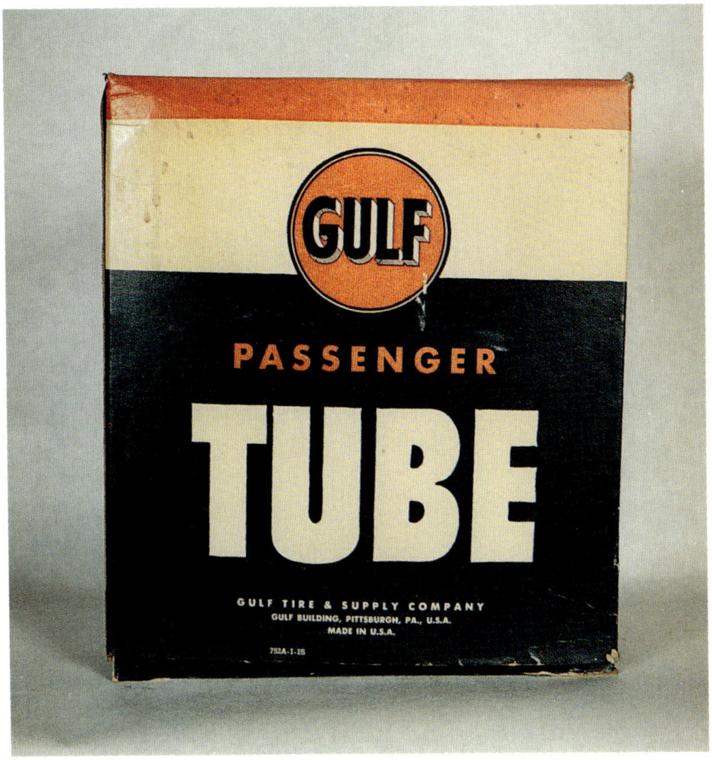


Tube and box, 1958, value $35.

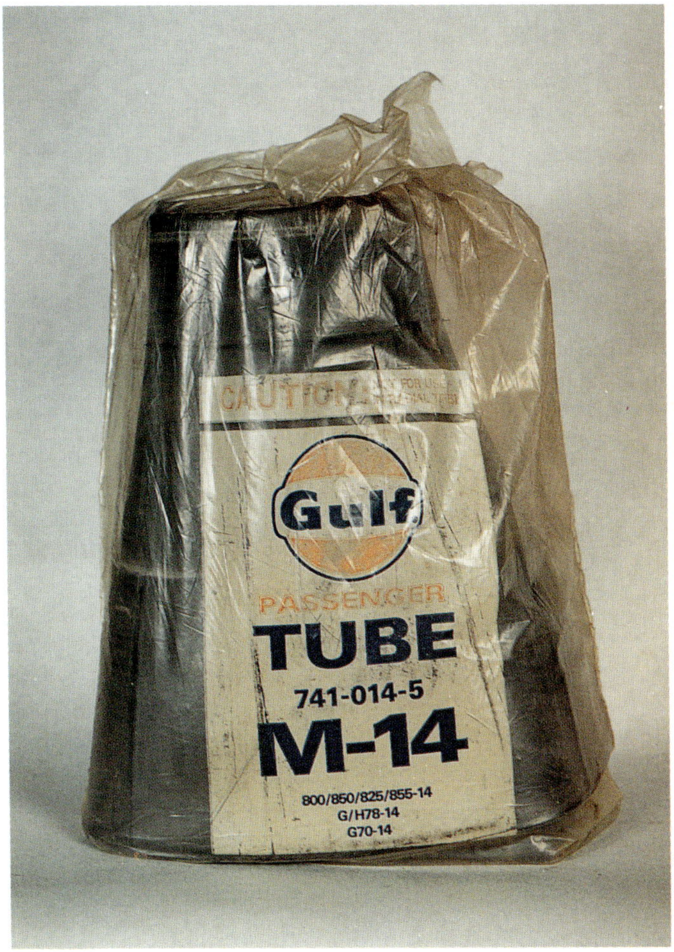


Tube and plastic bag container, 1984, value $20.

Tubeless tire repair kit, value $50.

Boxes for seals and patches, value $20 each.

Left to right: 1940, 1940, 1950, 1962, 1950, value $100 to $150 each.

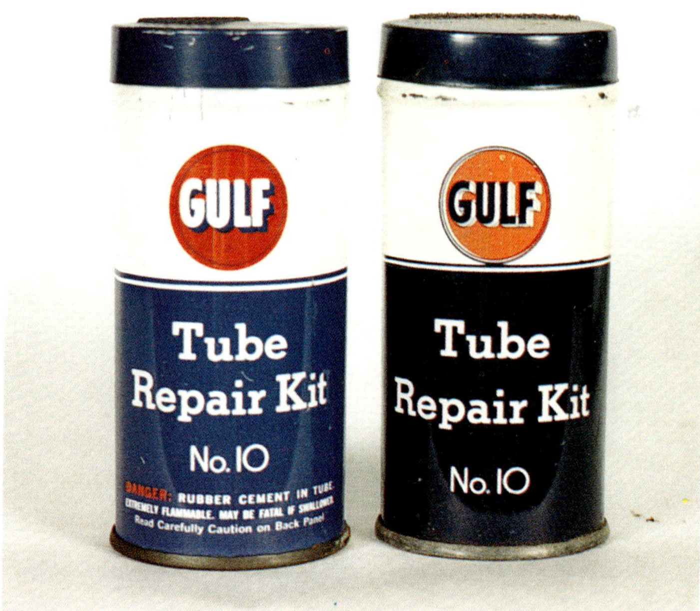


Left, 1962, value $40. Right, 1950, value $50.

Left, 1962, value $40. Right, 1968, value $40.

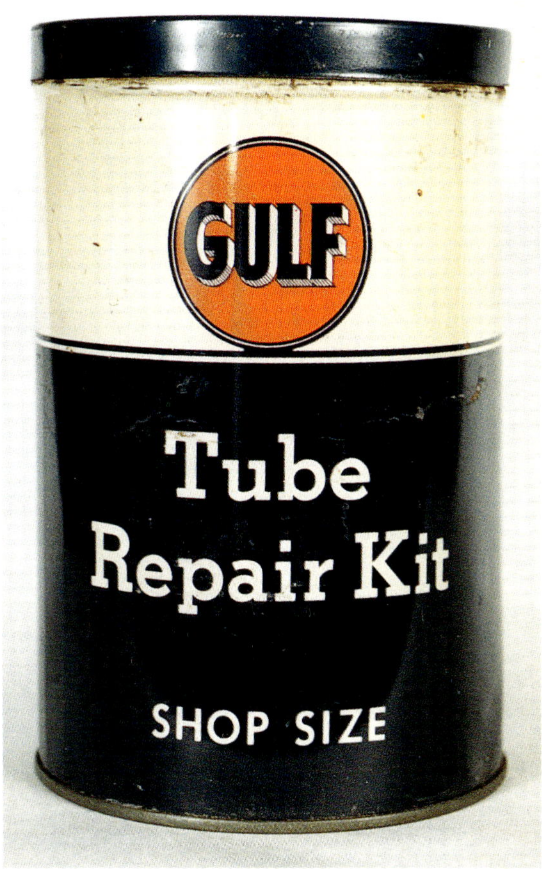


Metal, 1962, no value established.

Tubeless tire cement, both valued $15 each.

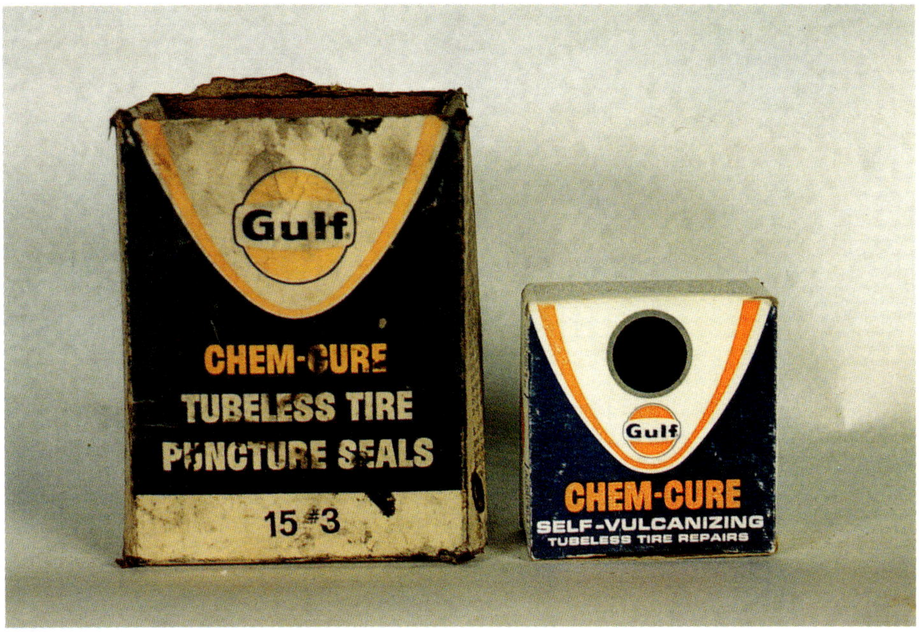


Tire seals, 1974, value $5 each.

# Utility Bags

Plastic bags, 1984, no value established.

Utility travel bag representing University of Louisville shown front and back side, value $45.

# Valve Top Oil

Pint, 1942, glass, value not established.

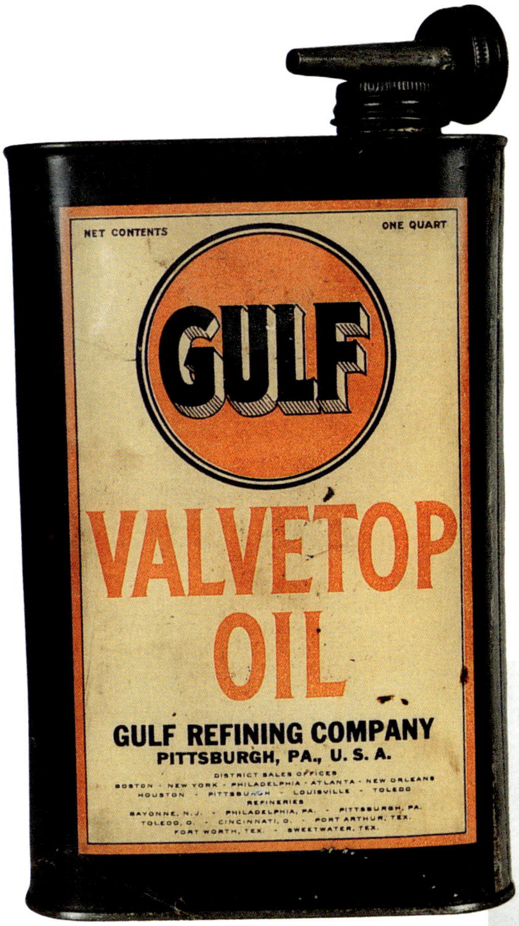


Metal, quart, 1940s, value $50.

Metal, pint, different and unique logo than other 1957 versions.

Metal, pint, shown 1950, 1957, 1964, value $20 each.

# Watches

District distributors award watch, value not established.

Watches of various types, value from $40 to $1. Note, watch to right is a reproduction, value $10.

# Wax Gulfwax

Paper box, one pound, 1920s, value not established.

Left, one-fourth pound, 1940s, value $25. Right, one-pound, 1940s, value $25.

Left, one-fourth pound, 1950, value $35. Right, one-pound, 1951, value $40.

Left, 1953, one-fourth pound, value $25. Right, 1964, one-fourth pound, value $25.

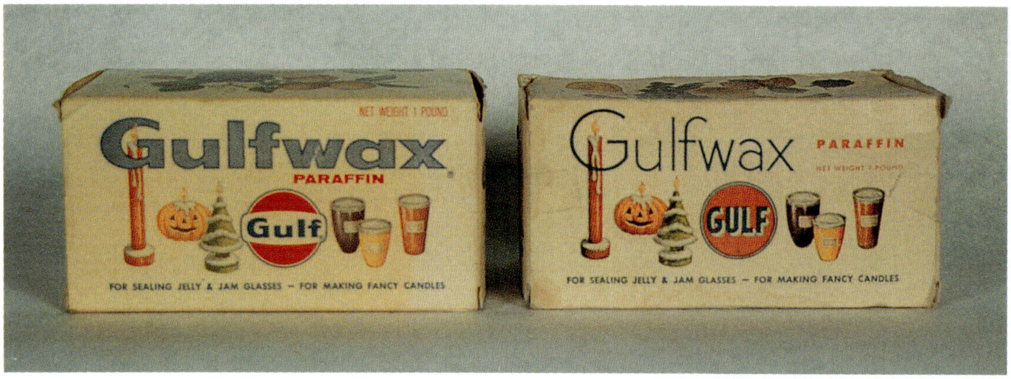


Left, one pound, 1983, value $10. Right, 1958, one pound, value $30.

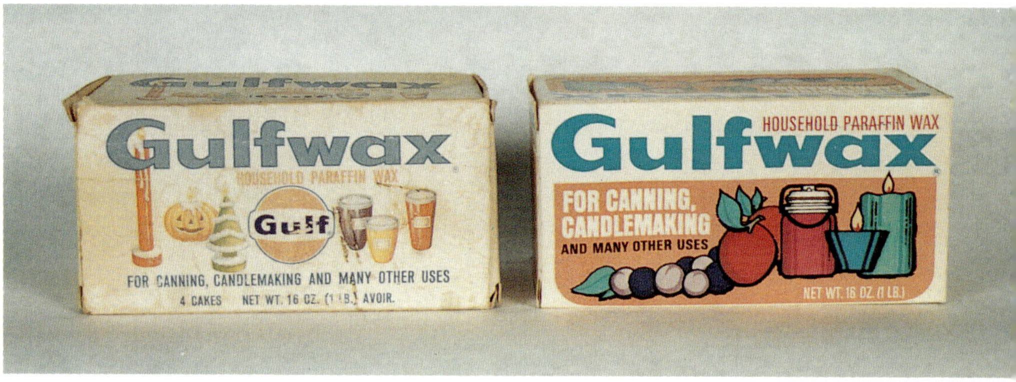


1990 versions, value $5 each.

## Wax Treated Dusting Cloth

Metal can with cloth, 1952, value $40.

## White Sidewall Cleaners

Metal, one gallon, 1958, value $70.

Metal can hand-pump sprayer, value $40.

## Windshield Wiper Blades

Display case with wiper, 1984, value $20.

## Window Cleaner

Left to right, 1973, 1970, and 1966, value $15 each.

# Appendix

## Trade Publications

Petroleum Collectibles Monthly
411 Forest Street
LaGrange, OH 44050
(216) 355-6608

Check The Oil
P.O. Box 937
Powell, OH 43065-0937
(614) 848-5038

## Appraisals & Buyer of Gulf Oil Items (Only)

Charles Whitworth
P.O. Box 4073
Jeffersonville, IN 47130

## Gas Pumps, Parts, Restorations and Petroleum Related Items

Vic's Place
124 North 2nd
Gutherie, OK 73044
(405) 282-5586